# In Search of... customers!

**Brian E. Butler**
&
Jennifer Vondenbrink

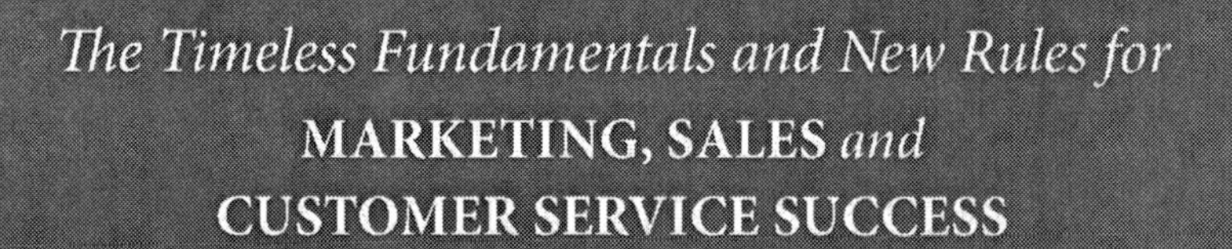

*The Timeless Fundamentals and New Rules for*
**MARKETING, SALES** *and*
**CUSTOMER SERVICE SUCCESS**

In Search of…Customers
The Timeless Fundamentals and New Rules for Marketing, Sales and Customer Service Success

v1.0



Outskirts Press, Inc.
http://www.outskirtspress.com

ISBN: 978-1-4787-7139-5



PRINTED IN THE UNITED STATES OF AMERICA

# Dedication

This book is dedicated to all the businesses (like ours) that have been strategizing, searching, and experimenting in response to the explosion of change during the last few years so they can remain viable and find new ways to provide value to their marketplace. No matter what you're looking for, students, patients, customers, clients, shoppers, members, donors, etc., we hope this book helps you find, get, and keep more of them.

# Acknowledgments

We'd like to say thank you to everyone who has helped contribute knowledge and insight into this endeavor. This would include all the teachers and mentors from whom we have learned, all the associates who have helped us deliver our services to customers, and the clients with whom we have worked in order to bring these principles to successful outcomes.

# Table of Contents

# Introduction

Surely by now, we can all agree. It's not our father's (or mother's) marketplace any more. And, unless you know something I don't—it is *not* coming back.

There has been a seismic shift in how business development works, and there is no debating the significance of the impact it has had on us all. We can see, feel, and experience the changes every day just by waking up and turning on our computer. The business environment that many of us grew up in is gone forever, never to return. And the rate of change continues at an exponential pace, forcing us to run ever faster to keep up. If you agree with that concept, what are the changes we all need to make to succeed now, and in the future?

I recently came across a version of the classic Washington Irving short story, *Rip Van Winkle.* You know the plot. Living in upstate New York around the time of the American Revolution, Rip, the henpecked husband, goes up to the mountains for a bit of respite and falls asleep for a period of 20 years. And upon awaking, finds a quite different world than the one he left. His adjustment and "catching up" period to the new world he is confronted by leaves him both happy and confused.

Can you imagine if the same thing had happened to us and we "fell asleep" during the last 25 years, only to awaken a decade or so into the new millennium? How far behind would we be? We would have missed the Internet, e-mail, blogs, cell phones, iPhones, iPods, MP3s, CDs, DVDs, DVRs, webinars, pod casts, social media, spreadsheets, and many other inventions of techno-wizardry.

In essence, we would have missed most of the fundamental and complete changes in the way we work, communicate, and entertain ourselves. Economic situations, demographic changes, world events, consumer expectations, increased competition from all corners, and many other trends only exacerbate the effect.

We have a sign that we hang at all of our sales meetings. I think the quote is originally attributed to Microsoft founder Bill Gates. The sign says: *When the rate of change outside the organization is greater than the rate of change inside the organization—the end is near!* The message is clear—keep up or get out! And the message is equally valid for both, organizations—and—individuals. As each of us are our own personal services corporations, we can't afford to leave our development up to anyone but ourselves so we can continue to deliver value to the evolving business landscape.

As the macrobusiness climate has changed, so to have the "rules" of marketing, sales, and customer service changed. Old school is often just that: old, tired, and ineffective in creating results. So the obvious question becomes, how do we grow our businesses now, given all the challenges we face on a daily basis?

The answer lies in linking your marketing, sales, and customer service efforts into a high-powered, coordinated business development engine. You must eliminate your silos, divisions, and internal politicking to attain dynamic and sustainable growth.

Picture a stool. You can be supported quite comfortably on one that has three legs. But have you ever tried to support yourself for any length of time on a stool that only has two legs? If you have great marketing that helps you find customers and a great sales effort that helps you get customers, but an inadequate customer service effort that does not allow you to keep what you've gained, what have you got? Or, if you have good sales production and convert most of your opportunities and good customer service and keep almost all that you earn, but marketing does not drive enough opportunities to sustain your organization, what have you got? A one- or two-legged stool will only get you so far.

Having all three functions of your business development effort, marketing, sales, and customer service up to speed is positively not a nice-to-have but an absolute must-have to compete, survive, and succeed. It does not matter whether you are a one-person practitioner of any kind or a multinational corporation.

Our attempt here is to combine those elements that are truly timeless and considered business development fundamentals with the strategies and tactics of modern social media. In this way, you can develop both a sustainable and steady stream of new opportunities and increase your existing customers' satisfaction and loyalty.

Someone once said that business is the thing that, if you don't have enough of, you go out of. Don't let that happen to you. If you need to attract, acquire, and retain more of whatever you consider is your revenue source, come see how things are done successfully now . . .

# Marketing-Rule #1

*"The aim of the business is to create customers"*

~ Peter Drucker

It is a fact so simple and yet so often overlooked . . . If the goal of business is to make customers, then logic dictates that businesses need to engage the marketplace relentlessly, *marketing* their products and services to specific target audiences. It is only in the creating of awareness, generation of interest, and influencing into action that causes people to spend their money with a particular organization or for a particular product, service, or cause.

The first Rule of Marketing is to make money.

You might have great brand awareness, the highest click-through and open rates, the slickest direct mail piece, the most award-winning advertisements, the best trained staff, the fastest whatever, and the latest and greatest product, but none of it will count unless certain combinations of these things help create customers and profitable revenue.

Feel free to experiment. Things that work for you today will not work tomorrow. If you've gotten lower results from your trade shows, try direct mail. If response rates on direct mail are down, try some new forms of advertising. Develop a content marketing program. Speak at industry events. Get your website up to date so it helps generate real leads.

But above all else, measure for results. Results matter. They are, in fact, all that matter.

In a marketing textbook, you'd likely read that marketing management is an *intentional* effort to control the exchange process of goods and services. And that it includes analysis, planning, strategies, and tactics implemented to create beneficial exchanges for the purpose of attaining organizational objectives. Or, more simply put, *making money!*

Don't be fooled by the "magic bullet" marketers. Or become too enamored with the latest technology. One single thing is rarely the answer. Successful business development is usually built on the back of a well-constructed marketing effort based on research and tied to organizational goals. A degree of innovation along with a solid, regular marketing program which helps differentiate your offering to your target audience, along with a well-constructed sales process, is usually the only sustainable competitive advantage in the long run.

Marketing creates customers. Customers create money.

Today, that well-constructed marketing effort needs to include some form of social media such as platforms (i.e., Twitter, LinkedIn, Facebook, Instagram, Pinterest . . .), blog, e-mail distribution lists, websites, etc. Without creating a company digital footprint, your potential customers may not realize you exist.

When was the last time you Googled something? Yesterday? This morning? An hour ago?

## Marketing—Rule #1

According to Internet Live Stats (http://www.internetlivestats.com/google-search-statistics), "Google processes over 40,000 search queries every second on average, which translates to 3.5 billion searches per day and 1.2 trillion searches per year." That's a lot of people looking for information. Many are seeking solutions to problems, some of which your company may be able to solve. To do so, however, they must be able to find you.

Not only are they doing searches, but they are reading blogs, asking questions on Twitter, checking out websites, and finding recommendations on Facebook, Yelp, and Google. Because of this shift in behavior, marketing looks different. Your message can't be "Buy My Stuff" or "Sale! Sale! Sale!" Instead, it needs to become more educational and relationship based. Honestly, that can feel uncomfortable for many of us baby boomers who grew up on Coke and Pepsi commercials.

In the end, they hope to find resources who provide quality information helping them solve current and future problems. You show value by helping them. Your message translates through the information. The better information you provide, the more you build. The more they trust you, the more they return. The more they return, the greater chance they will buy.

If you want to create a sustainable competitive advantage, part of your marketing investment must be on a serious social strategy which does not mean someone occasionally posting to Facebook. It is an intentional effort. There is that phrase again, with a clear message, call to action, and follow-up.

A well thought out, integrated, traditional and social marketing strategy allows you to create ongoing qualified leads who come to the table much more prepared to purchase.

# Marketing Defined

*Marketing: a. The act or process of purchasing in a market. b. The process or technique of promoting, selling, and distributing a product or service*

~ Merriam-Webster online

*The process of planning and executing the conception, pricing, promotion, and distribution of ideas, goods, and services to create exchanges that satisfy individual and organizational objectives.* -American Marketing Association (AMA)

*The minimization of the hindrances that keep your key audiences from using your products, services, and/or ideas, and the maximization of the "helps" that make it easier to use them.* - David Marlowe

*Eight factors that combine to create the facilitation of selling products and services between parties: price, people, product, placement, promotion and education, productivity and quality, process and physical evidence* - Unknown

## Marketing Defined

Ask a dozen marketing professionals and you're likely to get a dozen different answers to the question of "what is marketing" based on their own individual experiences. Here is mine, which is assembled from several sources using language that speaks to me.

> *The never-ending process of creating strategic plans and specific tactical actions done intentionally and consistently to influence the perceptions of a target audience or individual buyer to investigate, evaluate, and ultimately, purchase your product or service to create, maintain, and/or grow revenue.*

That's truly a mouthful. I often get too wordy. But all of it is important in this case.

Here are the words that are important to me in this definition and some thoughts on each.

- *Strategy*—Simply put, this is determining the "who are we trying to sell to" and the "why are we trying to sell to them."
- *Tactics*—This is the what, where, when, and how of marketing.
- *Intentional*—In just about all hospitals, there is an accident room that generates some patients for the institution. But very often, that is exactly the "business" that the hospitals don't want. There can be issues with admissions, free care, and the ability to pay. In most cases, "accidental" business is something we should try to avoid in our organizations as well. If we accept this kind of business so easily, very often, we find we have to service what we really don't want to have, leaving us no time to pursue the kind of customers we really want and need.
- *Consistent*—If you've ever been on a diet and/or exercise program, you know that if you don't keep at it every day, you will not achieve your goal. We're not surprised when we skip the gym too many times or go for the "candy-bar-a-day" instead of

the "apple-a-day" that we don't lose the weight or get in shape. Yet, we sometimes scratch our heads in amazement that when we only market sporadically, more business does not come our way. A commitment to healthy living makes us healthy. A commitment to marketing makes both our top line and bottom line healthy.

- *Influence* (perceptions)—Influence in marketing is developing the ability to alter or impact the thoughts, ideas, behaviors, and actions of your prospective customers. Specializing in something and becoming an expert at what you do are the quickest ways to create the highest levels of influence.

As we begin to think about our integrated marketing efforts, it is important to consider each of these points as they relate to traditional and social tools.

Here are some questions to ask as you move through these bullet points.

- Why are you selling what you are selling? If you don't think understanding your why is important, check out the TED Talk by Simon Sinek, "Start with the Why." https://www.youtube.com/watch?v=sioZd3AxmnE.
- What do you want to be known for? How would you like to influence your audience?
- Who is your ultimate customer? What do you know about them? What do you need to know about them?
- Where do your customers hang out online? It does no good to create a Twitter strategy if your customers aren't there, even if it is integrated with your traditional media.
- Speaking of traditional media, what forms of media do your customers use? Have they gone paperless or are they

still responding to paper-based marketing? What about radio and television? Are they still active users in traditional media or have they transitioned into newer versions such as Netflix, Pandora, and Amazon Prime?

- What matters to your customers? Are they eco-friendly? Are they trendsetters? Are they late adopters? Understanding these facts allows you to develop marketing that matters to the customer and keeps them engaged.
- What is the next step you want them to take? Most campaigns, both traditional and social, fail because organizations spend all their time creating the content or marketing materials without a thought of what steps do they want the customers to take. By storyboarding the process, you can clearly identify next steps and chart results.
- When and how will you communicate? West Jet did an amazing holiday promotion carefully orchestrated both in traditional and social media. They surprised customers with Christmas gifts told to Santa prior to boarding their flight. When they landed, not only did their luggage appear, but so did a load of individually wrapped and tagged gifts. The video release on YouTube was timed with press releases to traditional media sources, company blog posts, as well as well staffed Twitter and Facebook administrators to handle all the comments. According to the Shorty Award Statement, "With the support of a strategic communications plan, YouTube views and media impressions far exceeded program objectives, contributing to an unexpected and unprecedented increase in sales during the holiday period." Check out all the results here along with the video. Be warned, tissues are required. http://industry.shortyawards.com/nominee/6th_annual/iK/westjet-christmas-miracle-real-time-giving.
- What tools will you use to ensure you deliver consistent online and off-line messaging? You can't show up just once and think everyone saw your message. You need a delivery

plan like *The Boston Globe*. You want to show up on time with the most important information so your customers come to rely on you.

- Who will create the content? Do you include customer-created content?

These are just some questions to get you started thinking about your integrated marketing strategy.

# Start at the Beginning

*"The dictionary is the only place where success comes before work"*

~ Vince Lombardi

When we say recite the alphabet, we always start with a, b, c . . . When we count, we begin with 1, 2, 3 . . . Every race has a starting point and ends at the finish line. Why, then, do we get so ahead of ourselves so often in our marketing efforts and try to rush to the end without even beginning the right way? There is one simple rule to follow to get all things marketing in the right order.

Strategy comes before tactics.

When playing Monopoly, we don't start at Park Place, Boardwalk, or even Baltic Avenue. We always start at GO. When we get things out of the proper sequence, often we don't achieve the desired outcomes. Missed steps lower our chance to win or even participate in the game.

Too often in the eagerness to launch a new product or because of a sales downturn, we rush to market with things that are inappropriate or "not ready for prime time." The company who is so caught up in its product design ability, yet puts no thought into who will want (and buy) their brilliant new invention, usually comes up woefully short of hitting their goals. In this case, experience will not meet expectation.

There are, of course, exceptions. But better to not expect that you have the next "pet rock" that will take off and sell beyond reason, no matter what you do. You don't put the horse behind the cart, and then whip the horse when the cart doesn't move.

In 1957, the Ford Motor Company launched what proved to be one of the costliest product disasters of all time. The name has become synonymous with product failure. The Edsel. The tactics used to attract attention to the new automobile were highly successful. On September 4th, eager consumers flooded the dealerships in record numbers. Company executives were ecstatic . . . until they understood that while many people came to look . . . very few ended up buying.

What happened? It appears, in Ford's desire to build excitement around the new car, they overlooked some very crucial factors that, if they had been paying attention, would have led to a completely different strategy. The tactics used to create "buzz" were very successful, but the hype did not live up to the reality of the product.

The expectation of a radically new kind of car was dashed when the public saw it, and they concluded it was more of what was already out there. Despite evidence that even at that time the public was beginning to be interested in smaller cars, especially while entering an economic downturn, Ford plowed forward with another large car. Even though extensive surveys and research indicated that people liked names like Corsair and Citation, Ford moved forward with a name (Ford's only child) that meant almost nothing to almost everyone.

Ongoing mechanical problems for those who actually purchased the car cinched the deal. Ford eventually pulled the plug on the Edsel to the tune of a $250 million loss in 1958 dollars.

Tactics must support the strategy. Strategy must support the overall mission. The marriage of tactics and strategy has to be like the old game show *Match Game.* By finding the most correct connection, you create the best chance to win the game.

By putting tactics ahead of strategy, you often put your passion ahead of your common sense. As Harvey Mackay said in his book *Swim with the Sharks*, "Make decisions with your heart and you'll end up with heart disease." Sometimes, the best strategy is to stop before you start.

Social marketing, specifically, is fraught with people jumping in because they think they should, without a thought to strategy or tactics. Setting up a Twitter or Facebook page does not constitute a social media marketing or marketing strategy, in general. Neither does setting up a LinkedIn company page, and then walking away 6 months later because things got busy.

Using social media platforms, writing blogs, tweeting, etc., are all tactics. They are only one step in the process that relies on strategy to drive it.

But to use these platforms effectively, it may take some relearning on the part of your organization. You can't transfer a web or print ad into a Facebook post. Well, you can, but it will not give you the results you desire.

The original intent for this new media was communication; thus, the phrase, social network. There were designed to create two-way dialogue between people. As companies and brands became involved, they evolved to marketing tools. That didn't change the intention. Ultimately, it is still about the conversation.

That is why ads don't work unless they spark conversation. Traditional marketing strategy was one to many. Tools and tactics were developed that facilitated this type of communication. It worked, and in many cases, still does.

In social, however, the strategy needs to shift as we have been discussing. The premise no longer is about what the company wants to shout to its followers; it is more about what the followers want to learn and know.

Therefore, think strategy first. Answer the important questions before diving into a social. As my mother would always say, "Think before you speak."

# Back-to-School Marketing

*"Education costs money, but then so does ignorance"*

~ Sir Claus Moser

Every year, all of the moms (and/or dads) of school-age children see and wait excitedly for the "big yellow bus" to roll down the road. It makes me think about what back-to-school lessons we should be reminded of from a marketing prospective. Here are three quick ones from various school subjects.

1. Science. All marketing is experimental. As any good scientist would say, discovery usually only happens with experimentation. What we once knew (or worked) gives way to new methods by finding newer, better ways of doing things. Different messages and different channels become more effective than the old ones. Marketing that works best now includes multichannel tactics such as digital, mobile, and social. Our understanding of what works changes in time. Nothing lasts forever.
2. History. That said, those who don't learn from history are doomed to repeat it. When things are economically challenging, as they have been for a while now, the unfortunate trend is for businesses to pull back from their marketing efforts. For

those who study, they find that this is always a losing idea. Historically, the most successful companies pour more into marketing efforts in a downtime. They find that their message gets more attention because there are fewer messages out there. And that leads to both, more opportunities and customers.

3. Physical Education (PE). Many a gym teacher with a whistle has extolled the virtues of being active. Couch potatoes are usually neither healthy nor successful. One gym class a day as a student or an occasional trip to the YMCA as an adult does not make or keep us healthy. It is the consistent, sustained effort over time that keeps us in the best physical condition possible. In the same way, one postcard, trade show, or other "quick fix" efforts are not the recipe to long-term marketing success and revenue growth. You have to get, and stay, in motion, every day, forever.

My kids sometimes say to me, "Why are we studying this stuff? We'll never use it in real life. It doesn't make any sense." If you look a little closer, it always does.

I remember making similar remarks when I was in school. For me, it was in physics. I am thankful my senior-year physics teacher had patience with me. I believe I wasn't interested because I couldn't see the value. I wasn't going to be measuring the speed of things or figuring out the torque of something, so why did I need to learn it?

When you don't see value in an action like tangible results, you lose interest. Like me with physics, you may feel the same toward social marketing. You know you have to be there, but because the barrier to entry is low, personal investment and interest can be low. Soon, you become distracted by other priorities and you stop posting, blogging, or engaging with your audience, like I stopped going to class.

Of course, hindsight is 20/20, and now I understand the importance of physics and leverage the knowledge I gained. Unfortunately, you don't have a decade or so to learn these lessons in business. As we said before, Marketing needs to generate Customers, but we need to understand how to utilize the Marketing Tools to achieve that result, and that may mean going back to school.

I don't know how social and digital marketing will evolve, but I know it will. If you are not willing to maintain a studentlike mentality and engage consistently in the process of measure, analyze, learn, adapt, move forward, you will never graduate with new Customers. Today, entire industries that resisted social are already seeing the decline of new customers less than a decade since the change began.

Things rarely revert to the previous generations. The Beatles didn't start playing Swing Music because that was popular in the past, nor did Glenn Miller play Ragtime. As much as you may want things to be like they used to, you need to move forward. It may be time to become a student again. There's a lot you may be missing.

# How to Earn an "A" at Marketing

*"Education is the best provision for old age"*

~ Aristotle

If the quote from Aristotle is true, then we should all strive to get A's in all of our educational endeavors. Here are some suggestions how to get A's where it counts—learning how to get more customers through "smarter" marketing.

*Absorb*—Good markers pay attention to everything. They notice the advertisement on the side of the bus. They actually go through their "junk" mail looking for trends and unique offers. And they actually read some of their spam e-mail. They do this because they know that they have to be on guard against and aware of what the competition is doing. And, good ideas sometimes come in the unlikeliest of places.

Just because someone else tries some creative marketing methods doesn't necessarily mean that they are appropriate for you. But if you are like a visual, auditory, and kinesthetic marketing sponge and "soak up" as much as you can, you just may find yourself in the position to capitalize on things others will overlook or ignore.

*Action*—I think it was hockey great Wayne Gretzky that once said, "You will miss 100% of the shots you don't take." In marketing, the correlation is you will not win 100% of the business you don't try for. Just as delay in a executing a military campaign to win a battle is often fatal, so too is indecisiveness when it comes to launching a marketing campaign to win a market. If you think you can capture a market, then you must act quickly. Other competitors probably have discovered the same opportunity as you.

Your marketing plan, which includes all of your communication "contacts," is wasted unless acted on. Don't let it become like a set of New Year's resolutions, made with great intentions, followed through on only sporadically or, even worse, not at all.

*Advocate*—If you don't love your product, who will? Marketers must love their brand, their products, or their service offering. You must be untiring, unrelenting, passionate advocates for your organization.

With the same tireless energy, you must "sell" internally, creating enthusiasm about your company where it sometimes counts the most, with your own people. Make sure your internal marketing and communications about company events, happenings, and successes don't go unnoticed.

*Ask*—". . . and you shall receive." Perhaps you've heard of the concept? Of all the things that are typically left out of an otherwise good marketing piece, the most common is a compelling offer. At some appropriate point in the prospect contact mission, if you do not ask for them to *do* something, you're placing all your good efforts in jeopardy.

A call to action, or at least an invitation for a prospect to "put their hand up" and request more information, delays or derails your marketing engine. It does not necessarily (nor probably should) include asking for the order at this point. Your list might include: download our white paper, come in for a test drive, drop by for a free sample, send for our complimentary evaluation, etc. Interest is required for engagement. Engagement is necessary for consideration. *Consideration expects an offer*. An offer is often needed to get action. Action is required for buying.

*Attention*—Latest estimates I've seen conclude that in America we see over 3,000 advertisements and over 600 marketing messages *every* day. But very few actually work their way into our consciousness. With all of the bombardment for our attention, you had better have something truly eye-catching and attention-grabbing in order to break through the clutter we usually ignore.

Great products, remarkable service, and cutting-edge technology will do you no good if your audience does not know about you. Your marketing effort, in whatever form you choose is appropriate and effective, must first create awareness. Then, and only then, will you have a chance to engage a prospect in the buying process.

*Authority*—One of the fastest ways to gain credibility with your target audience(s) is to display and promote your expertise in your industry or product and service. All things being equal, people will often, if not most of the time, choose the "expert" to do business with. If you have individuals or business processes that are clearly superior to that of the competition, play them up.

Write white papers, give a seminar, be a guest columnist, appear on a talk show (or even write a book!). Work hard to be the best at what you do. Then, turn on your marketing machine and make sure your prospects and customers know how they can benefit from your expertise.

These take hard work, planning, and systems in place to make them happen. "But," I hear you say, "I don't have time."

## How to Earn an "A" at Marketing

You have the same 24 hours in a day that your competition does. How you use that time is up to you. Here are some suggestions:

- First thing in the morning, grab a cup of coffee and jump on Twitter, LinkedIn, or check out RSS feed tools like Feedly to catch up on daily and industry news.
    - Make note of interesting things about which to write.
    - Make note of interesting things your competition is posting.
    - Note any new trends.
    - Share interesting articles to my followers.
- Weekly touch base with five LinkedIn connections.
- Publish a weekly (or if that feels like too much, bi-weekly or monthly) article on LinkedIn. This could be taken from your morning strolls through Twitter.
- Notice what catches your attention. Make a note of it. Why did you share that article? What made you click on that link? What did you find interesting about the video you just spent 2 minutes watching? Why did you download that white paper? These are all clues to why your customers might take a similar action with your content.
- Spend time weekly checking out what the competition is doing.
- Find some companies or individuals who are successful using digital media to market their products. Follow them. Notice what they are talking about and how they do things.
- Attend local or national Inbound Marketing or Digital Marketing Conferences to better understand how to use the media and make connections.
- Test different calls-to-action on various social platforms. Measure results and adapt.

- Engage, and possibly educate, your entire organization in the marketing effort. Today, unlike years ago, if you aren't building advocates within the organization, they could be undermining your online branding and marketing efforts by what they are posting, unprofessional profiles, etc. Your customers aren't just looking at the business page; they are also looking at the individual behind the scenes. Starbucks does a fabulous job of this on Twitter. Follow the hashtag #tobeapartner and look at how they engage all levels of the organization as advocates for the company.

Can you do all of these every day? No. Can you start to build them into your daily work flow? Probably yes, starting small and gradually increasing your efforts.

# Start Every Day Shiny

*"You never get a second chance to make a first impression"*

~ Will Rogers

Late last year, some road work and a construction inspired me to change my normal route to work. Not wanting to wait for alternating turns to go on a four-lane road that had been condensed down into a one-lane road, I took a much-longer distance route but thoroughly enjoyed the flowing traffic. The new path brought me past a large local car dealership. Since it was before 7:00 a.m. each day, I did not expect to see much if any activity as it was well before normal working hours. What I saw, however, really got my attention. And in the end, I was surprised what it caused me to do.

In the lot were three different two-man teams, each with buckets and sprayers attached to garden hoses, washing off the 200 or so cars parked in neat rows across the expansive parking lot. There was no visible evidence of any trees nearby or falling leaves. There were no wires where offending birds may have been perched. No new snow, ice, or any other kind of precipitation had occurred in weeks. Despite the absence of anything that could possibly soil the car exteriors in any way, I noticed how meticulously each and every car was being cleaned so that when the prospective customers came to the lot that day, each vehicle would look its absolute best. And each and every morning for the weeks I traveled that particular route, I saw the same procedure and process happen.

It reminded me once again that everything that every organization does is marketing. Either you are making yourself look more attractive, or less attractive, to your customers and prospects. There is an undeniable power that comes with every first impression. All perceptions originate there. You might have the best strategic marketing plans possible, but if your execution leaves the product unattractive or less "shiny" than it could be, you are creating a disadvantage for yourself and your salespeople. The perception created by those random drive-by trips for me? Simple. It created the feeling for me that this dealer paid attention to details. That that business dotted their i's and crossed their t's.

Marketers and business owners need to always make sure that the lobby is neat, the rugs are vacuumed, the bathrooms clean, the light bulbs all work, and that the marketing messages are clear, all in alignment, and that they are delivered in both a timely and consistent fashion. Salespeople, make sure your shoes are shined, your teeth brushed, your attitude positive, your sales literature organized, you ask lots of questions, and that you leave whoever visits you or you visit feeling better when you walk out than when you walked in.

Even when you don't know they are looking and observing, potential customers are checking out and paying attention to the unintended marketing messages you are sending out. Sales are often made on first impressions as they create a powerful set of expectations in the mind of a customer about both the kind of experience and service that he or she will receive. Given that, make sure to put your best foot forward in all the ways that customers may see and evaluate you.

P.S. What did that car washing/attention-to-detail dealership cause me to do? At that particular moment in time, I was in the market for a new car. An unforeseen event had created an unexpected opportunity. Despite having another vehicle all picked out, I decided, based on the favorable yet unintended marketing impression they had created, to give them a shot. And I ended up buying one of their "shiny" cars instead.

Your online presence is just as important as vacuuming, dusting, and putting on a clean shirt to meet a customer. Unfortunately, due to the low overhead of engaging on the social channels, far too often, profiles and accounts are set up and something happens to draw company away. It could be another platform, product launch, or something as simple as the person who set up the accounts no longer works for the company.

Customers do not care what is happening behind the scenes. If they are in the market for your products or services and they come across your old Facebook page that hadn't been updated since 2014, they are going to move onto the next guy, your competitor.

With all there is to do in a day, where do you start to polish your online presence to a high gloss shine?

The first step is to conduct an online audit of your company which is as simple as doing a Google search with your company name. Note all the social platforms you are listed on.

Second, create your content. Before you go dashing off to fix this or patch that, take a moment to gather your tools. The car washers wouldn't be nearly as effective in washing the cars if they had to keep running back and forth for their buckets, hoses, etc. You shouldn't be doing that either.

Instead, craft a summary of yourself and your business, making sure to use the keywords your customers use to find you. Find the image or images you want to use across your platforms. Make sure you have the correct web address and the web addresses of other sites you want to link to. These might be other social media profiles, blogging sites, or different divisions of your company.

Armed with your tools, go forth and clean. A unified image across your social media platforms assures potential customers you are ready for their business.

# Don't Go Hunting without the Right Weapons

*"A man who stops advertising to save money is like a man who stops a clock to save time"*

~ Henry Ford

In every Robin Hood movie I've ever seen, one of the common moments is when the famous outlaw shoots a second arrow at a target that splits in half the first one already there.

I'm guessing chances are when Robin went hunting he didn't miss much. With that kind of aim, he could most surely take down a rabbit or deer or boar. When shooting arrows, specific targets, with good technique and skill, make both for good hunting and full bellies.

In the modern business development parlance, a hunter is someone who is supposed to go out into the (suspect) prospect forest and always "bag" the new customer. But what if the hunter has no arrows in his or her quiver to shoot with?

In business development, roles, expectations, and perception are critical. The role of marketing, with the assistance of product development, is to give the hunters (or sales force) as many arrows—advantages, benefits, and value propositions—as possible. Most hunters don't necessarily need superior products or the lowest pricing, but, there is really no way for them to hunt successfully with an empty quiver.

Marketing is the weapon of sales and business development. Unlike in times gone by, it is marketing and not sales that is most responsible for initiating the customer relationship. Almost no one can or will know about you without consistently delivering content that both educates and influences potential customers into action. Why, then, do so many organizations only "dabble" when it comes to creating and delivering marketing materials and other support tools?

If you are not arming your hunters with the specificity of who or what you want them to bring back, and why, chances are you're going to get something different for dinner than what you wanted or expected. This equals level-one qualification of the correct prospects or potential ideal customers. This is not necessarily easy work and usually requires much time and effort. But trying to skip or cut corners on this step probably equals no dinner.

While the prey in the forest may not decide what kind of arrow they want to be shot with, today's customers do. They are way ahead of hunters these days in terms of prequalifying what kinds of companies and individuals they want to do business with. Websites, LinkedIn, and similar online tools make this a reality. Content is a large quiver, or maybe a snare, that ensures that prospective customers get to know you on their terms. Build your supply of case studies, white papers, blog posts, etc., and make sure you distribute them plentifully and frequently in the prospect forest.

At the end of the day, the mission is accomplished and the victory is won with the proper tool that gets the job done. Knowing what the key drivers are in a prospect's decision-making process and what problem you're solving are crucial. Compelling offers, differentiated products and services, testimonials, references, easy-to-try-and/or-buy methods, and clear, consistent messaging go a long way in helping your hunters and sales force bring home the right customers.

You don't use a cannon to kill a mosquito. You don't use a butterfly net to catch fish. The right tools are critical in accomplishing just about any task in life. Make sure if you are going to market to commit to supplying your team with the right weapons to help entice prospects and create customers.

My grandfather was a fisherman. Nothing special, and far from professional. He was more the pick-up-his-old-pole-and-head-out-on-the-lake type while on vacation. He would tell us what type of bait worked best or what types of lures to use and why. As a kid, I thought he was born with this magic knowledge, not realizing the hundreds of books he must have read in the off-season.

He did his research, just like you need to do your research when building your quiver full of content arrows. When we defined marketing, we talked about various questions to ask prior to developing your marketing strategy. These questions will also inform what type of content to develop, calls-to-action to compel your customer to act, and in what forest or social platform you may want to begin to cast your content net.

Think of these arrows as providing your potential customers with the information they need to solve a current problem, while placing a seed of knowledge about your expertise and business. With each arrow, the seed grows as does their trust and confidence in you.

Let's take the story of Gary Vaynerchuk, an entrepreneur who took his father's liquor store from $3 million to $50 million in annual sales over the course of 7 years. How? Every week, he produced his own video called Wine Library, where he talked about wine, but not in technical wine terms, but in language everyone could relate to. Then he got on social media and engaged with his audience, answering questions and giving people advice about wine.

By providing regular content that was accessible to the audience he wanted to reach, he built an audience who turned into customers. He didn't do everything on every channel. He answered the marketing questions, got to know his audience, and gave them what they wanted. They, in turn, became loyal customers.

# Build a Pipeline Not a Funnel

> *"Authentic marketing is the art of identifying and understanding customer needs and creating solutions that deliver satisfaction to the customers, profits to the producers and benefits for the stakeholders"*
>
> ~ Philip Kotler

Maybe we have one in the garage for when we add oil to the lawnmower. We've certainly seen one on a thousand PowerPoint slides or sales and marketing textbook pages. The funnel. And we expect our lead generation results to work like the funnel does in real life—pour something in the top and get something out the bottom just about right away.

But real lead generation does not work that way. Oh, you might get a small percentage of "immediate" business from a direct marketing campaign, trade show, or other activity. Like many things in life, it might fall into the 80/20 split of short term vs. longer term. Chances are much greater that it will take a sustained effort over an extended period of time to build a true lead generation engine for your business. More like a pipeline. Building a structure and tapping into fertile fields that deliver a steady stream of opportunities is always better than pouring in random chances from various places.

Consider the Trans-Alaskan pipeline. I suppose it could have been an option to send someone with empty barrels into the oil fields and try to fill them one at a time. But thankfully, someone had the good sense and engineering ability to build something that has functioned at a very productive rate over a long period of time.

But there were certainly lots of obstacles to overcome. Consider that to build the pipeline,

- It took a long time. Over 4 years to build.
- It had to cover a great distance. Over 800 miles.
- It was done in a harsh climate. Last time I checked, Alaska was very cold.
- It had to be constructed over rugged geography, mountains, and fault lines.
- It took sophisticated engineering. Pipes had to be elevated and the oil heated and pumped.
- It required lots of manpower. Over 21,000 people in total.
- It had to overcome the "natives." Herds of thousands of wandering caribou.

The question to ask is at the end of all the time, resources, and money—was the effort worth it? Well, when you consider that since 1977, the pipeline has delivered over *20 billion* barrels of oil, the answer becomes quite obvious!

Successful lead generation is exactly the same. To get the maximum value, you must build a system that will have something (prospective customers) in it at all times, not just when you are ready to pour something (buy now) in it. Prospective customers can not all be sold when you're ready, but, many more can be brought along at their own pace and eventually come out the end with a sale than by just going for the immediate result all the time.

In a recent discussion with a B2B lead expert, he mentioned to me the following statistics that were compiled after a long study in several industries. On average, of the 100 percent of people who will buy from you at some time after the initial contact or inquiry from a prospective customer, only 25 percent buy within the next 3 months. Only 20 percent more buy during the first 9 months after first contact. After 18months, 25 percent more will buy, and fully 30 percent will take more than 18 months to consummate a first-time order. That means that *over 50 percent* will take more than 9 months to come to a buying decision after first contact.

When viewed through the pipeline philosophy, the importance of persevering over an extended period of time becomes more evident. Your lead generation activity and efforts are like a preview of coming attractions for prospective customers before they decide to buy from you. We'll talk more in the next two chapters about what you should do and how you should handle the prospects you want to keep "in your pipeline."

You might one day get in a lucky shot like Uncle Jed did in the opening sequence of the classic TV show *The Beverly Hillbillies* when he missed the rabbit, hit the ground, and up came the "bubblin' crude." But by building a carefully crafted marketing and sales pipeline, you will generate better and more consistent leads and create more of the right customers in the long run.

Including social in your marketing efforts not only allows you to generate leads, but it comes with a change of behavior. You cannot only put up what you want to sell. That is like flashing a neon light in their window 24/7. After the first night, people either move or find a way to avoid you.

Putting up pretty pictures also will not work. Sure, people may like what you're sharing, but after a while, they get bored. Without something to invoke interest, you become noise in the background at best and a forgotten connection at worst.

To build a pipeline on social means you need time. Not the answer you want to hear because last time I checked, no one had invented the 36-hour day.

Nevertheless, you need time. You need time to engage with the people who follow you, answer their questions, find out what they are talking about, comment on, or share their content.

You also need time to create good content that speaks directly to your potential customers. This could be blog posts, LinkedIn articles, presentations to share on SlideShare, or videos to upload to YouTube or Vimeo.

You need time to curate content your potential customers will find interesting. According to News Cred, the average company with a content strategy is creating 65 percent original content and curating 35 percent.

Finally, you need time to create compelling calls-to-action. Gone are the days when "Like Us on Facebook" was unique enough to get a response. Customers today are building their own channels for news, industry updates, entertainment, etc. In order to get them to click here, you need to give them a pretty good reason why.

Yes, that is a lot of time. Yes, that is a lot of effort. I'm sure it feels like you are building your own Trans-Alaska Pipeline. In effect, you are, only the oil is content flowing to your potential customers.

# Draw Smaller Circles

*"Go first to those you are sure will buy"*

~ Benjamin Franklin

Ever found yourself in a friendly game of darts down at the local pub? If you have, when you were lining up your throw—what were you aiming for? Hopefully, if you are playing to win—you were throwing for the bull's-eye.

Now ask yourself this question, "Why do we throw the dart at the bull's-eye?" Answer—we get the most points by hitting the center. Hitting the center of just about everything gets you the most points and helps you win whatever game you are playing.

If we are trying to win the game of marketing, then—we must know where the center is for our efforts and what makes up the "game board" to begin with.

Very few of us or our businesses are going to sell to "everyone." There are only so many McDonald's and Walmarts. For the rest of us, it makes infinitely more sense to aim more precisely and target our energy, focus, resources, and messaging to those prospective customers we conclude are Most Likely to Buy (MLB) our product or services.

In Jim Collins's classic *Good to Great*, he talks about the Hedgehog Concept. In the intersection of three characteristics lies the secret of great organizations: what your economic engine (what makes you money) is, what you have passion for, and what you can be world-class at doing.

The "Rule of Three" seems to exist in other areas as well. In military terms, it is having superior power in air, land, and sea forces. In winning baseball teams, it is having the combination of pitching, hitting, and defense.

Truly effective marketing is made up of three parts as well. Consider these three factors: the right target, the right message, the right offer.

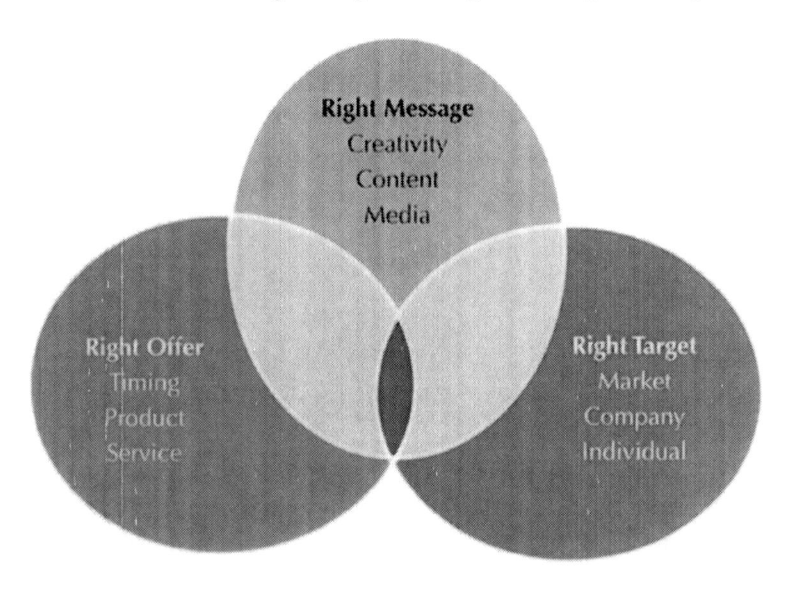


Think back to the example of business development. When you only have two legs of a three-legged stool, you have one very uncomfortable and ineffective device. If you only have two of the factors in effective marketing—you haven't got much either.

Have you produced an award-winning creative piece delivered to the exact audience you wanted it to go to but not had a compelling or relevant offer that helped people "put their hands up" with interest? Have you ever generated lots of leads or sales by sending a good message and a good offer to the wrong target? Bad aim is not good marketing. To score points and win the game, you must get the right information in the right people's hands at the right time.

Missing the dart board and hitting someone in the butt with a well thrown dart is not going to accomplish much either. Except maybe to start a fight.

When you understand your target audience, it is much easier to determine the right message and the right offer. So, do you know who you want to target, whether it is using traditional or social marketing?

This can be one of the most challenging parts of the marketing process. Choosing one target market to speak to, at least at the beginning, feels as if doing so will limit your success. It increases your chance of being heard.

What you want to do is create a profile of your ideal customer, a buyer persona. HubSpot defines a buyer persona as:

> "a semi-fictional representation of your ideal customer based on market research and real data about your existing customers, including customer demographics, behavior patterns, motivations and goals."

Some of the key characteristics to include are:

1. Age

2. Level of education
3. Marital status
4. Where does he/she live?
5. What do they do for a living?
6. How much do they make?
7. What are their hobbies or interests?

Then you might want to take it to the next level with questions like:

1. What are their life goals?
2. What are their career goals?
3. What types of media do they consume?
4. Where do they hang out online and off-line?
5. What activities are they involved in?

Why do you need to know all this information?

Because each point helps you craft your message or show up in the right places on social to engage with your ideal potential customer. By understanding these and even deeper questions, you are better able to speak the language of your customers, thus, gaining their trust.

Let's take an example of an estate appraiser. Their initial marketing campaign was to share their estate sales on Twitter and Facebook. They saw some results but nothing much. In the process of developing their buyer persona, they realized their ideal customers were hanging out on Twitter during *Antiques Roadshow*. This insight allowed them to develop a marketing campaign they ran, including a short Tweet Chat after *Antiques Roadshow* to answer questions. Brilliant!

This is nothing new. Marketers have been doing this forever. Why do you think people advertise during the Super Bowl? They know their audience is there. Who shows up? Coca-Cola, Doritos, Chrysler, Anheuser-Busch, BMW, Discover Card, P&G, McDonald's, just to name a few. You don't see ads for Chia Pets or The Clapper (you know, "Clap on. Clap off." The Clapper.) Why? They certainly could advertise if they had the money, but it might not be the best investment if their audience wasn't watching the game.

Understanding your target, message, and offer are foundational to any marketing campaign. It is an important step that, if missed, results in your efforts becoming the noise instead of the message your customers need to hear.

# Don't Play Pin the Tail on the Donkey

*"Before you build a better mouse trap, find out how many mice are out there"*

~ Mortimer Zuckerman

We've all played the game, right? Perhaps it was as a child some time ago. Or maybe it has been at your own child's birthday party in the last few years. And it never fails to deliver the laughs. You stick the picture of the tailless donkey on the wall. You blindfold little Johnny or Susie, and then spin them around for good measure. Then you turn them loose in a futile attempt to pin the tail on a donkey they cannot see while they are slightly disoriented. More often than not, the tail gets pinned on a curtain or the side of a chair or sometimes the backside of the unsuspecting host.

Another party favorite that is similar is the birthday piñata. While blindfolded, children (and sometimes, overzealous adults) swing a bat wildly at the candy-loaded character hanging from the ceiling or tree in an attempt to break it open and get the candy. Everyone usually laughs and usually wins at least some candy.

## Don't Play Pin the Tail on the Donkey

How often do we treat our marketing efforts in exactly the same way?

Have you ever sent some postcards to "lots of people" *hoping* somebody will respond? Have you ever attended trade shows without being certain exactly who would be there?

Do you know exactly who your customers are and why they buy from you? And just as importantly, do you want more of the same kinds of customers or different ones?

The fact is too much marketing is done with the "leap before you look" philosophy. We put tactics ahead of strategy and do things that are counterproductive to what our goals should be (that is, if we know what they should be at all).

The only way to build a winning marketing program is to know exactly what target you're aiming for—and—where that target lives.

Just like hitting a target you cannot see, the odds of winning business by "shooting in the dark" are not high. Ready, Aim, Fire does not work anymore. It takes serious investigation and a multidimensional marketing effort to earn business consistently in the twenty-first century.

Commit to these three precampaign ideas to define your goals better.

<u>Survey Current Customers</u>. It can be by phone, fax, e-mail, direct mail, or personal interview. Ask what they like and dislike about you and your competitors. What features or advantages are they looking for ideally in your product and service? This builds goodwill, conveys sincere interest, and earns extra business.

<u>Conduct primary research</u>. From time to time, contract with someone to help you understand more about your industry's trends and buying preferences. Insights will prove to be invaluable. Conditions that you understood yesterday and when you made your sales are not the same

today and will be different tomorrow. Being able to spot changes will allow you to know not only where the targets are, but also more importantly, where they will be in the future.

Create Customer Profiles. Use information technology to analyze the characteristics of your customers, both the ones you want more of, and the ones you don't want at all. This can assist in making intelligent, informed decisions about products, campaigns, strategies, and tactics before you commit to launch. Develop personae of each of your customer segments so that you can tailor your marketing messages to each individual group. This increases relevancy. Increasing relevancy increases the number of responses. Increasing the number of responses increases your odds of converting more customers.

Successful marketing is not child's play. Next time you go to market, lift the blindfold.

To stay relevant in today's changing environment, conducting research not only before you begin a marketing campaign, but continuing your research day to day is vital.

Since 2004, Facebook has gone from 1 million users to over 1.18 billion daily active users and has acquired Instagram, Atlas, WhatsApp, and Oculus. Looking at their history timeline, there are dozens of launched features many users don't even know exist. Facebook is only one platform out of hundreds worldwide, each with a slightly different focus and audience.

You need to understand the changing nature of how your audience is using a certain media. Take the news, for example. If you are 65 or older, you probably tune into your television to watch the evening news on a regular basis. If, however, you are 22, you rarely tune into the news at its appointed time. Instead, you turn to your social networks to find out what is happening. If you are in the news biz, this is important information.

Facebook is always experimenting with the algorithms of what is shown in user's newsfeeds. In this offical post (https://www.facebook.com/business/news/update-to-facebook-news-feed) on November 14, 2014, for example, Facebook outlines changes for 2015 regarding overly promoting page posts. Basically, if you were going to be screaming "Buy My Stuff" all the time, they weren't going to show it to the people who liked your page. If you weren't keeping up on such changes and planned similar posts for your Facebook Business Page in 2015, you would be disappointed in the results.

Basing your marketing plan on rumors and half-truths can be a costly effort. Companies exploring data once as it relates to their campaign may not be aware of current updates. This results in wasted time, money, and potentially lost or never reached potential clients.

A better strategy is to research and continue to monitor the channels you use, as well as your demographic for changes. Doing so will provide you and your marketing team with the most relevant information for them to make informed decisions and create marketing plans with impact.

# Place Your Bet

*"Those who are victorious plan effectively and change decisively"*

~ Sun Tzu, *The Art of War*

I'm not much of a gambler. Biggest chance I usually take is to buy a $2 lottery ticket when the jackpot gets high enough. But I am hopefully smart enough to know that when it comes to marketing, playing it safe is not necessarily playing it smart.

One of the more common errors that can be made when it comes to your marketing and contact strategy is to think that you can "cover all the bases" effectively. Just as you cannot sell everything to everyone, you also cannot market multiple messages to the same target group or the same message to numerous target groups. Only confusion will ensue about who you are and what you stand for.

Almost all organizations are confronted with challenges that require either expanding the product line or discovering the need to diversify into new products or services at some point in their existence. The most common reaction to this is trying to keep a foot in both camps, but that is usually the decision that makes the least sense. By trying to focus on everything, you'll end up specializing in nothing.

Jack Welch, legendary CEO of General Electric, knew this when he made his proclamation that "We'll be either number one or number two in the markets we serve, or, we'll get out." He understood that you must make a commitment of time, energy, and resources to win the game, and that if you spread yourself too thin, you end up being average at everything and excellent at nothing.

Few, if any, organizations have the ability to be attractive to all potential customers. Your marketing, graphics, language, content, offers, etc., represent your magnetism to potential customers. You will attract some people—and—repel others. That is OK. Sometimes you may be tempted to play it safe and cover all your bases in an attempt to maximize your odds.

Playing it safe often doesn't mean that you're playing it smart. It's like going into the casino to play roulette and putting a chip on odd and even, black and red. You'll get to play the game, but you can't win anything. At some point, if you want to get ahead, you're going to have to place your bet where you may lose, but, at least, you have given yourself a chance to win.

Here's an example. A small marketing company started out wanting to help business with all aspects of marketing. They wrote blogs, created social media posts, developed print ads, wrote press releases, designed websites and more. Because of their talent, their work got noticed.

Over time, it became clear doing these different things didn't allow them to focus on their core competency, developing catchy campaigns. They made the decision to change their messaging to reflect this focus.

Amazing things started to happen. They got focused on who they wanted to target for new business and potential partnerships. From those efforts, very quickly, came opportunities to quote larger jobs. Larger marketing agencies took notice and began to include them in large proposals.

Bottom line, they received more business based on their core competency than they ever could have trying to be everything to everyone.

The baby boomer generation grew up in the marketing era of getting the word out to as many people as possible, broadcast marketing. It works well if you are a large brand with several channels and large marketing budget, but for the rest of us, the better we can focus on our core competencies, communicate our advantage, and speak the language of our audience, the easier it is for us to cut through the noise and be heard.

Here's a great exercise.

Think about your core marketing message. Why do you do what you do? Who do you serve? How do you best solve their problem?

Next, distill that message down to 8–10 words or one sentence. Even better, try to do it in under 140 characters. Then, test the message on social, in your print marketing, and when talking to other people. Notice the difference in their reaction.

As Albert Einstein said, "If you can't explain it to a six-year-old, you don't understand it well enough yourself."

# Marketing Is a Lot Like Riding a Bike

*"If you can't fly then* ***run****, if you can't* ***run*** *then* ***walk****, if you can't* ***walk*** *then* ***crawl****, but whatever you do you have to keep moving forward"*

~ Martin Luther King Jr.

I came across the picture recently of the day my youngest rode her bike for the first time. I remember it clearly as Annie, age 7 at the time, rode her bike with no training wheels attached. Having done this seven times previously, you'd think I'd experienced everything that could be learned about this particular moment of parenthood. But that was not the case.

Her older brother actually got the tools out and helped me take the training wheels off. We suited her up with the obligatory helmet, elbow and knees pads, and let her have at it. I explained that she could go as far as the driveway three houses up the road and the driveway two houses down the road. To which, thankfully, she promptly agreed. So she began, and then also promptly fell down.

Along the course of the next 25 minutes or so, she alternatively fell, wobbled, swerved up on neighbors' lawns, and almost ran into two mailboxes and one telephone pole. She quit several times. She threw the bike down other times and had several tantrums that would make any frustrated 7-year-old proud.

Eventually, of course, she got steadier and steadier, and by the end of a half hour or so, she had it down. She could start up and keep going on her own, and although all the lines were not straight, she began to easily get from point A to point B.

And so it dawned on me that learning to market yourself and/or your business is a lot like learning to ride a bike. There are four things that seemed remarkably similar to our experiences every day at work when we try to help our clients attract more customers.

1. It's OK to start small. Biking begins with training wheels. Marketing begins with the basics. Make sure your collateral, business cards, website, etc., all look professional and appropriate for your target audience. Think of these essentials as your starter package, the small bike with training wheels . . . necessary to have to begin the journey.
2. But you have to get in motion. Owning a bike is fun, but they are not built for you to just sit on in the driveway. They are made for motion and travel. Think of marketing as a verb. Not passive, but rather, active. At some point, you have to get your name, materials, offers, etc., into the hands of potential customers, or they will not know that you are an option to buy from.
3. Set goals. Going from mailbox to mailbox is a good start for riding a bike. Learning to get started from a stopped position and riding in a straight line are parts of it. A certain number of pieces mailed, e-mails sent, phone calls made, or other SEO or automation (for advanced riders) metrics are worthy of your time and attention.

4. Don't quit. All too often, we hear from clients that their marketing efforts "just aren't working and we're going to stop for a while." Well . . . If, after every time you fell down when learning to ride a bike, you quit, you may still not know how to ride one. Falling down and making mistakes are just part of the learning process. Marketing, and learning to ride a bike, are both experimental. You can only succeed by staying with it.

Get out of your comfort zone (and neighborhood). Eventually, as you become more competent on a bike, you'll go past the mailbox and the last neighbor's house and eventually onto a main road and another destination. To be a Tour de France rider, you have to go on a long journey over mountains and unfamiliar territory. To become a successful marketer and get new customers for your business, you'll have to target those outside of who you know, and who know you, and find a way to reach them. Just like the first time riding a bike without training wheels, it may feel uncomfortable, but doable if you stick with it.

I remember learning to drive for the first time. Although I had been a passenger in a car thousands of times, the first time I pressed the accelerator down and felt the car lurch forward, I felt out of control. I jammed on the brakes, panting with relief that we didn't hit anything. I felt like I could never master getting the hang of driving, but here I am, years later, driving around like it's the most natural thing in the world.

Social media marketing can make you feel the same way. You are learning a new skill. At first, it is going to feel uncomfortable. It is going to take practice, persistence, and education. Your first Twitter post will feel silly. You will stare blankly at Facebook wondering what to post. You will fiddle around with Instagram, wondering how in the world will this work for me.

Go back to the crawl, walk, run model. I do not agree with the directive you must be on every social channel to be effective. I think that is like learning to ride a motorcycle instead of a bike. If you fall off a motorcycle, it is much more dangerous than if you tip over on a bike. The same is true on social.

A better approach is to begin with one platform. Install training wheels in the form of education. Don't assume the intern from college has the expertise your organization requires to implement social as part of your marketing plan. Instead, dive in and get your hands dirty. Remember, this is your voice, your brand, your reputation on the line.

Once you have one platform under your belt add another. Again, learn it. Understand it. Develop a strategy for it.

Social media marketing isn't limited to the marketing team or person. It's not just a sales tool. It's not just for HR to use for recruiting. It is a whole company initiative. That is why a slow, steady implementation is important from the ground level up to the executives.

Just like any skill, biking, walking, or doing a triathlon, no one jumps out there the first time and does it perfectly. In fact, there are a lot of baby steps that need to happen to get up to speed. When you began to walk, you looked at each tumble as a learning event. Apply the same crawl, walk, run attitude to your social media marketing, and you will be in shape for the marketing marathon in no time.

# Avoid Marketing's Bermuda Triangle

> *"To what extent are you truly changing perceptions, buyer behavior, attitudes, loyalty and the like?"*
>
> ~ Joseph Jaffe

The Bermuda Triangle conjures up images of mystery, danger, and disaster. All too often, marketing gives the same feelings to those who don't understand it or have failed at it.

Most frequently defined as the area between Miami, San Juan, and Bermuda, the "unexplained disappearances" of both ships and aircraft in and over those waters have stirred the imagination for over 60 years. Previously referred to as "The Deadly Triangle," the phrase "the Bermuda Triangle" was popularized in a 1962 article titled "The Mystery of the Lost Patrol" by Allan W. Eckert. Later, in 1974, a best seller from Charles Berlitz that sold over 5,000,000 copies in hardback pushed the Triangle to true cultural phenomenon status.

Though much debate still rages over the circumstances and validity regarding the mystery of the Bermuda Triangle, no such mystery exists over the "unexplained disappearances" of sales and customers due to falling into marketing's Bermuda Triangle. Just as three points always make up a triangle, these three marketing mistakes create an area where profits and progress can be swallowed in a "perfect storm" of sales prevention.

1. We know who our customers are. Living in deeply parochial New England, we all too often hear something along the lines of the familiar refrain, "But we've always done it that way." This dedication to the ostrich method of marketing (or management by sticking your head in the sand) when it comes to not acknowledging changes in technology, styles, or buying behavior is extremely dangerous. Or, the opposite but equally effective business killer, "Everyone is our customer." Though I've seen some Mercedes and BMWs on *my* trips to the local Walmart, I'm pretty sure that even they do not expect to have *everyone* as their customer. In an era of ever-increasing specialization, the need to define your target audience is no longer a nice-to-have but an absolutely need-to-have requirement.

We worked recently (after the initial agency) with a very popular local tourism client that was dismayed and perplexed over the ineffectiveness of a recent series of campaigns to increase membership. They had targeted the kind of families they had seen every day at their organization. They could not understand when the carefully created graphics with the equally carefully crafted message used across a wide spectrum of media did not have the hoped for impact. They knew *for sure* who their customers were because they saw them every day.

Only after some careful digging in the database and questioning was it discovered that while young families did attend in big numbers, they *were not* the customers who bought the memberships. In this case, it was actually the *grandparents* of these families who purchased memberships as gifts for their grandchildren, yet the initial campaigns completely ignored this group because of the original insistence of *knowing* who the new customers they hoped to attract had to be.

2. We don't need (or can't afford) marketing. No less an authority than the late business guru Peter Drucker said that all businesses had only two priorities: innovation and marketing. He also commented "The goal of marketing was to know and understand the customer so well as to make selling superfluous." Sounds not only important but mission critical to me. Yet, marketing is often the first thing to be cut (if it exists at all) in a downturn or when companies feel the need to reduce costs. How dumb is that?

Not doing something to attract, or even worse, making your prospects *aware* of your existence, is no recipe for success. I've seen statistics that estimate that we see on average over 3,000 advertisements and over 600 marketing messages *every day*. With that much competition for your customers' and prospective customers' attention, doesn't it make some sense that you not only have to be part of what they're seeing, but even more importantly, find ways to break through the clutter and get noticed.

For almost every organization who doesn't invest in marketing strategies and work to woo new customers with a multifaceted marketing program, the end is inevitable, and . . . maybe sooner than they think. The hypercompetitive marketplace we all live in will simply not allow for below-average performance. Natural selection will eventually take over and doom some organizations to extinction. Other competitors will eventually copy most products and services, and your advantages will slip away. A degree of innovation along with a solid, regular marketing program which helps differentiate your offering to your target audience (along with a solid sales process) is usually the only sustainable competitive advantage.

3. Engaging in "pixie-dust" marketing. The other reaction in a downturn is to say something like, "Quick, let's do some marketing to get sales up." TV commercials from not that long ago advocating that Yellowbook advertising is the "cure-all" to a bad sales month or quarter only serves to reinforce this type of thinking.

But rarely, if ever, does a one-hit marketing effort drive results, and even if it does in the short term, it's highly unlikely to do so over the long run. *Marketing is not an event.* One trade show, one postcard mailer, or one person dressed up as a gorilla standing outside your store is not likely to make much of a long-term impact. Successful business development is usually built on the back of a well-constructed marketing effort based on research and tied to organizational goals and strategies.

Most of us like the escape of a good movie. We like to travel through time, fly off to strange lands, or engage in an epic battle of good vs. evil. Our daydreaming often leads to great breakthroughs. However, leaving the growth and revenue success of your organization to marketing "fantasies" and wishful thinking goes beyond being not advisable; it's actually downright negligent. Hope is no substitute for sound strategy.

Three points can make a triangle. Three points can also make a line that becomes a trend. No matter which configuration you put these three points into, "knowing" the customers you really don't know, not "needing" the marketing you desperately need, and engaging in silver-bullet thinking will only lead to one place. But unlike many of the "unexplained" disappearances of the Bermuda Triangle, if you employ this kind of business development strategy, the disappearance of your business will not be hard to figure out.

Too often, social, or marketing in the broader sense, is the silver bullet organizations try to employ as the sale "cure-all." Sales are up, no need to market. Sales are down, all hands (and tools) on deck, even if we don't have a plan or really know how to use them with today's consumer.

When marketing, and social media specifically, is used in situations like this, failure is inevitable, not to mention wasted time and money at a time when both are precious commodities.

Why?

Because if you don't know exactly who your customer is, then you do try to use it as a communication tool to everyone. You water down your brand message. This is the kiss of death in a society that moves from one thing to the next with a click, swipe, or scroll.

The other reason companies jump on board is because they don't have marketing budgets. It looks like a cheap way to "get the word out there."

Social is just as costly, and perhaps more when not structured, because it is a loss of time than just traditional marketing. Although you may not see dollars leaving the bank account, you will see decreased productivity and sales, because there is no measurable plan in place.

Bottom line is, if you want to use social, you need to prepare rather than just jump. You need to know your customers from all angles. You need to dedicate resources to the plan, including time and money. Finally, you need to establish goals to measure results.

# Marketing Is a Lot Like Parenting

*"Don't worry that children never listen to you; worry that they are always watching you"*

~ Robert Fulghum

Taken at face value, we know that our behavior as parents gets somewhat "off track" from time to time. As marketers, we need to be aware that customers actually behave in very predictable patterns (like children). It's our strategy and tactics that sometimes go astray. Job number one then is to develop a consistent process in order to *influence their behavior* in a way that facilitates positive results for both parties. Just like in parenting, we have two main weapons in our arsenal to carry out this battle. Nurture and relevancy.

Nurture. For any of you who are or ever have been parents or caregivers to children, I think you'll see where I'm going with this. As newborns through the toddler years, children are totally dependent on adults for protection, guidance, discipline, feeding, changing, etc. Our main mission is to nurture the development of these youngsters until they can begin some self-care and decision-making processes on their own.

Raising eight children, I have had more than my share of nurturing opportunities. In my rough estimation of my parenting career to this point, I have performed somewhere in the neighborhood of 8,000 diaper changes and north of 25,000 tuck in/kiss good night episodes. There are literally tens of thousands of potential interactions where we can imprint our hopes and desires into our children. Why do we do this? Simple. We hope that through these repetitive acts of kindness, that someday, we will have developed a meaningful and connected relationship. Effective nurturing is at the heart of successful personal relationships.

In just the same manner, we (should) nurture our prospective customers with information, offers, suggestions, and opportunities to learn how to make good buying decisions and demonstrate what success looks like by utilizing our product or service. If it takes thousands of points of contact to establish relationships in our personal life, why do we sometimes think that one or two postcards or meetings at a Chamber event will solidify a long-term client? It takes much more nurturing (communication) to initiate, develop, and grow business relationships as well.

Nurturing is the consistency and commitment to keep on keeping on with the intention of not giving up too soon. The old standard used to be five to seven "touches" before someone actually began to have an idea of what you did. The most recent research I've seen seems to indicate that now it's closer to nine contacts. And that's to just get in the door. Clearly, the nurturing effort in the business development process is not getting any less important either.

Relevancy. Later on, children turn into something called teenagers. Yikes. I once had six in the house at one time. There are many other wonderful books on that subject. I'll just take one piece here.

In our house if we want to, ahem, *motivate* the children to either do their chores or clean up their rooms, there is only one sure-fire remedy to get the results we want. Highly relevant rewards or the absence of rewards. For the 15-year-old, the incentive usually revolved around more computer time. For the 14-year-old, it usually drifted toward more TV time. For the 13-year-old, it could be more time with friends. And the 12-year-old was satisfied with more ice cream. I'm not suggesting bribes here, just the use of effective means to influence perceptions and stimulate action.

In just the same way, the era of mass marketing is all but dead. If your message does not totally answer the question, "what's in it for me?" you have almost no chance to be considered. Efficient and cost-effective marketing today must "drill down" to the specific wants and needs of individual buyers if you expect them to notice and take action.

As we've mentioned elsewhere, use the data you possess about customers and prospects in order to zero in on just those things that uniquely influence their perceptions and stimulate them into action.

Be prepared to nurture your business targets over the long haul and use relevant messaging to achieve the results you want. Just like raising good kids.

I was asked recently, "Can you build authentic relationships on social? Relationships that lead to sales."

The answer is yes, and even better than you could if using mass marketing. The reason is on social, you have opportunities to interact with those potential customers and get to know them. You also have an opportunity to discover their true needs.

Every year, we receive a mass marketed postcard from a local chimney sweep company. Each year the postcard goes in the recycling bin, not because I don't like the company, but we don't have a fireplace.

In this case, they are targeting home owners, but that is too general. Many of the homes on our street have fireplaces, but many do not or they do not use them. How would the chimney sweep company know this if all they do is send out postcards a couple of times a year?

Social media provides the opportunity to build and nurture relationships. If the chimney sweep company engaged the people on our street, they would understand who has fireplaces and who does not. Then they could target their message connecting deeper with those potential customers.

Social also provides another opportunity untapped by many who still hold a traditional mind-set. I honestly cannot tell you the name of the company because I barely look at the postcard on its way into the recycle bin. What if, however, they engaged me on social? What if they provided useful information for home owners beyond just your fireplace? What if I used their tips, and they saved me money, or helped me complete a project? Do you think I would remember their name then? Probably.

Social engagement is the new word of mouth. If I like your company, whether or not I can use your services right now, there is a big chance I will share your company with others who need what you do.

Here's another example of how social allows us to interact well before the sale. Let's say you met a potential customer at an event. You both agree it would be mutually beneficial to meet up again. In the past, you would follow up with some e-mails or possible calls before the meeting, right?

Today, with the help of social networks, you can magnify your touches building a relationship well before the meeting. Besides the e-mails and calls, you could invite them to connect on LinkedIn or follow them on Twitter. Before you meet, you can comment on their posts, review their history and their connections, and share their information with others. By the time you get together, you have established a relationship well beyond an initial meet and greet.

Remember, each of your potential customers has what they perceive to be a unique need. When you learn more about them through social, you can tap into that need, build a relationship, and whether or not they buy from you, create a brand advocate who becomes part of your extended marketing team, sharing what you do with their world.

# Marketing Can't Be Replaced

> *"Marketing requires data gathering, analysis, training, testing, and discipline—repeatedly if you want loyal customers and repeat sales. Sometimes you get lucky. But it's risky business to leave something as important as your company's livelihood to chance"*
>
> ~ John Hebert

For quite some time now, a big controversy has been going on with our local football team. The infamous "Deflategate" scandal surrounding Tom Brady and the New England Patriots. But prior to that, a few years ago, there was another utter disaster in the National Football League (NFL) regarding the use of replacement referees.

The NFL decided (which, in hindsight, proved to be very faulty thinking) to lock out the regular referees when the contract with the union expired. Thinking that it wouldn't make any difference to the overall quality of the game, the NFL brought in "replacement referees" to officiate the games. Instead of using the tried-and-true professionals that had been with the league for a very long time, the NFL went with referees from Division 3 and high school and expected them to perform at a level close to what the regular refs did. To say that it did not work would be a Titanic-sized understatement.

The powers that be in the league office decided that it was worth it to run the risk of the brand, or the "shield," as they call it in the NFL, by trying to save some money and not invest in something that was an integral (though believed to be insignificant) part of both the game and the overall "product." The ensuing fiasco ensured them a place on the front page of the paper, lead stories on talk radio, and even caused the league to be roasted on late-night TV.

The hue and cry built through the first 3 weeks of the regular season with good reason as easy calls were missed, games were slowed down to a crawling pace, and eventually, on a Monday night in Seattle, the outcome of a game was changed and defeat was snatched out of the jaws of victory with one erroneous call on the last play of the game. Instead of an interception being awarded to the Green Bay Packers that would have won the game, the play was ruled to be a catch and a touchdown for the Seattle Seahawks, securing the win for them.

Repeated television replays only confirmed what everyone knew right at the end of the game. The call was blown, and in an enormous way. Within 2 days, an agreement was reached with the regular referees and the "replacements" found themselves out of the limelight, their 15 minutes of fame over.

It occurred to me that there were three very applicable lessons learned from the NFL's handling of the matter from day number one of the lockout right up until the time a new deal was reached. Those lessons can easily be transferred to the current business climate and the fact that in far too many unhealthy ways, marketing has been pushed to the background.

1. What's it worth? In the NFL's faulty thinking, they assumed they could "get by on the cheap" and break the union and

employ new referees at lower dollars, thereby holding down the cost of officiating the games. What they found out is that sometimes when you try to cut corners, you end up watering down the product, losing and/or angering your customer base. It's like trying to sell a pizza with no cheese.

In the last few years of economic hardship, one of the most common things to go first on the chopping block had been marketing budgets, sacrificed because of the belief in some corners that you could get by without marketing. Those companies are almost always the hardest hit and take the longest to recover because of the thinking that marketing is not worth it.

2. Anybody can do it. With the explosion of social media and the desire (wish) to have it be a "one-size-fits-all" solution, too many people who are on Facebook think they are social media marketing gurus.

The reality is, marketing is still done best by marketing professionals who are cognizant and experienced in a variety of strategies and tactics. There are no silver-bullet/pixie-dust answers to targeting, approaching, communicating with, educating, engaging, nurturing, and ultimately, converting prospects into customers. Just like officiating an NFL game—it is better to leave it to the pros.

3. What's the real problem? Did the NFL have either a top or bottom line problem? Not at all. It was the envy of the professional sports landscape, a $9-billion industry that was (and is) the most popular sport in America. But the thinking (again), that some "cuts" could have no impact on revenue and reputation proved wrong.

Trust me, your salespeople have not gotten stupid or lazy overnight if you have a revenue problem. Most often, a sales problem is really a marketing problem in disguise. Proper marketing helps you figure out who your customer is, what they want, how to communicate with them, and how to create the conditions in which they will feel both comfortable and confident to buy from you.

Your lack of marketing, of telling your story to the right people at the right time, is usually the real problem. If you fail to tell a compelling story, you fail.

Remember, once again, Peter Drucker said that marketing and innovation were the two most important things in business, more important than even finances and operations. Just as there are no substitutes for good eating, rest, and exercise in order to stay healthy personally, there are no "replacements" to marketing in order to stay healthy in business.

I see this play out when a company wants to expand into social, so they do so by adding the responsibilities onto someone's already busy plate. Speaking at a recent conference, one of the attendees stood up and asked, "How much time does this social stuff really take? We're busy, you know. We don't have a lot of extra time (or funding) to waste."

I looked directly at the person and asked them what they did in their organization. Their function was a full-time job. Then I asked them how they were implementing social. Their answer was, "I do it when I have time. I know I have to, so I squeeze it in to get something out there."

This isn't uncommon. I cringe when I hear a company has hired an intern to handle their social or the receptionist/admin assistant loves Facebook, so they are handling social for us. That is the same as bringing in the replacement referees, and in many cases, for the same reasons stated above.

Social isn't something to casually pass off to a part-time or inexperienced person. It isn't a line item on a marketing plan that says something like "Twitter - Ongoing." Creating an integrated social marketing plan is a full-time job. It is probably one of the most important parts of your marketing plan because it is where you can interact with your potential customer base.

*"My store, Wine Library, outsells the big national chains. How do you think we did it? It started with the hustle. I always say that our success wasn't due to my hundreds of online videos about wine that went viral, but the hours I spent talking to people afterwards, making connections and building relationships."* ~ Gary Vaynerchuk

I mentioned Gary Vaynerchuk earlier. When he started Wine Library, he talked about working all day and engaging with his audience answering questions and being helpful, his social marketing strategy, well into the night. They became loyal brand advocates for Gary. He engaged. He showed them he cared. He invested quality time in his audience, and they returned his efforts tenfold.

Your organization can try to Band-Aid your social efforts, but will not drive results. It is not until you accept that social media is a professional part of your marketing efforts and bring in the folks to do the job who are qualified or spend the time educating your current staff, that you will make headway.

# The 10 Commandments of Marketing

*"Unseen and Untold equals Unsold"*

~ Unknown

1. Do let everyone you know what you do
2. Do not expect them to remember—keep reminding them
3. Do embrace marketing as a way of life and not as an event
4. Do not expect any one thing to be the only thing you'll need to do
5. Do give away information for free that builds your credibility
6. Do not give away all the answers—that diminishes your ability to be billable
7. Do use tactics that attract attention and give you the most return
8. Do not expect anything that works now to work forever, or maybe even awhile

9. Do measure all marketing activity for results that lead to revenue growth
10. Do not think you will discover all the answers—marketing will always be experimental

## Selling–Rule #1

*"At the end of the day we are not selling we are serving"*

~ Dave Ramsey

I went into a store recently that I do not usually frequent in search of a new suit. They had produced some eye-catching advertising and were offering what appeared to be some good deals.

Without much conversation, the salesperson I met had me try on something that he suggested would be perfect for me. I did not like the feel of the material. Though he suggested that it would be wonderful for the cooler weather that was coming, I did not like the cut of the suit. But he assured me that their tailor could alter it expertly. I did not like the pattern of the suit. The salesperson insisted that it looked great on me.

I walked out without buying anything and went back to my normal go-to store.

Rule #1 of selling is to make sure that your product, service, or offering is both a good and appropriate fit for your customer and meets their needs.

Qualification, the term most associated with this concept, is or should be a two-way street. A potential customer has to investigate and evaluate possible suppliers in hopes of finding one that can meet their requirements. In the same way, the best sales organizations don't take just any or all business. They are more selective and choose those customers that fit what their idea of what an ideal, or at least a good, customer looks like for them.

We may be able to sell someone once by providing something that they really don't want. But don't count on them coming back. Steven Covey, author of *The 7 Habits of Productive People*, taught many years ago the absolute importance in any deal or negotiation of creating the "win-win" arrangement. If we try to force something on someone that they don't need, the only long-term guarantee is a loss of both trust and credibility.

It is a salesperson's primary job to analyze customer requirements and propose potential solutions. Sometimes you may feel that you need to be creative in either approach or offer. That is acceptable, proactive, and worthy of praise. Just make sure not to offer slim fit jeans to someone who is looking for pleated and cuffed slacks. What you suggest needs to be close enough to a round peg in a round hole for the customers to appreciate your efforts to service them.

As for me, I went back to my normal store and have a new suit that I really like . . . and without a hint of buyer's remorse.

The social media experience you provide your customers is equally as important as their in-person experience. Your customers regard your online presence as an extension of your brand. If there isn't alignment, you may lose potential customer sales.

Case in point . . . I recently did an audit of my customer's social media sites. They hired an outside firm to post for them, and I wanted to check on the progress.

None of their sites reflected anything like the image the company hoped to convey to their customers. They were a more serious firm, and their online presence featured goofy videos, promotions of other products and links to other pages not aligned with the company. From the outside looking in, it didn't make sense.

I understand you want to connect with your audience. I even coach people to think about how they can make their online presence relevant to their audience and become what I call more 3D, but in this case, the dots didn't connect. Looking at their Facebook page, for example, I would have no idea what they did or what they could do for me as a customer.

Even though you may have several different solutions, you cannot be everything to everyone. Trying to do so makes you look like that overcompensating salesperson who only receives commission. In their eyes, you look good in anything, because all they can see are dollar signs.

We've recommended doing a social media audit earlier, but now go back and review your social presence with the eye of your ideal customer. Even better, walk through your social sites with someone new to your organization. Ask them what you do or what you sell. If they can't tell, it's time to do some work tailoring your messaging.

Selling Rule #1 is all about being the right fit for your customer in *their* eyes, not yours. They need to feel you are on their side in the sales process. They want to feel you understand them. The better you can convey this on your social channels, the more successful you will be engaging your potential customers, and ultimately, increasing sales.

# Selling Defined

*"Selling is not something you do to someone, it's something you do for someone"*

~ Zig Ziglar

The very best selling is never about selling. It is always about buying. Especially in the post-Internet/social media world. Buyers today are armed with too much information about the product or service they are considering. They do extensive research and know about the pluses and minuses, and quite possibly, even about you too. Salespeople are no longer in the advantageous position of having more, if not most, of the answers. Selling today is now certainly not pushing something on someone, but rather, finding how your product and service fits your prospect's requirements and helping them see that for themselves.

Based on that, here is my definition:

*Selling is the never-ending process of creating both the unique and appealing buying conditions that help enable each individual prospect, customer, or user into taking actions that ultimately lead to a purchase.*

Long gone are the days of the fast-talking and glib salesperson. Most buyers today can see through insincerity as easily as looking through a pane of glass. Even more so, they can *feel* if something isn't quite right or they are being pressured to buy and are more armed to quickly walk away from the situation.

Selling has become, and will only continue to be, more defined not by a salesperson's ability to "close the deal," but rather, the ability to understand the individual needs of each prospect, match up the value of their product and service to that need, and make it comfortable to buy.

We all like to buy things. That can be fun. We all hate to be sold things. We often feel taken advantage of and frequently lose trust in the person or company with that style of business.

Know which side of that equation you want to build your selling process on.

A couple of years ago, I wanted to buy my father an Internet-ready television for Christmas. Not knowing anything about the different models, I started my research online over the summer, checking out differences between televisions, features, etc. As fall approached, I got more serious. I looked at sizes, capabilities, longevity. Finally, as the holiday drew near, I researched where to buy the television. All of this was done online, through manufacturer, retailer, and review sites. The day I bought the television, I walked in the store, found a clerk, told him what I wanted, paid for it, and left. The whole transaction took less than 15–20 minutes.

I didn't buy because of the store's Black Friday Sale. I didn't buy because I got a flyer or an e-mail. I bought when I was ready. I knew what I wanted and how much I wanted to spend. I narrowed down my choices based on these criteria.

Did their marketing tools keep the store I chose at the top of my mind? Sure. Did they stop me from vetting the competition? Absolutely not.

Traditional sales and marketing tactics focused on SALE! SALE! SALE! Companies encourage you to buy when they want the sale, not perhaps when you are ready to buy.

Because today's customer has technology in the palm of their hand, they are in the driver's seat. Your customer is comparing you to your competition while they are in your location, at a meeting with you, or even standing in line with their purchase. You never had control over their buying decision; but today, your influence has to be more than alerting them of a sale. You must become a resource for them 12–18 months prior to their purchase.

Approximately 93 percent of B2B, business to business, or B2C, business to consumer, consumers begin their purchasing process with an online search. Layering traditional aggressive sales tactics on today's consumer will only end in disaster.

The key is to become customer-centric. Acknowledge your customers are in charge, and they will buy when ***they*** are ready. If you want your ideal customer to sit up and take notice, you need to provide a reason why and follow up with value. Do this consistently and you will be top of mind and top of their list.

# Put Away Your Battering Ram

*Tom contemplated the boy a bit, and said: "What do you call work?" "Why, ain't that work?" Tom resumed his whitewashing, and answered carelessly: "Well, maybe it is, and maybe it ain't. All I know, is, it suits Tom Sawyer." He had discovered a great law of human action, without knowing it—namely, that in order to make a man or a boy covet a thing, it is necessary to make the thing difficult to attain. If he had been a great and wise philosopher, like the writer of this book, he would now have comprehended that Work consists of whatever a body is obliged to do, and that Play consists of whatever a body is not obliged to do.*

~ Mark Twain, *The Adventures of Tom Sawyer*

"Buyers buy because of the way they buy." I heard that out of the mouth of Professor John Gockley at the University of Bridgeport during my junior year sales class at least once per night. The message he was trying to drill through our somewhat dull 20-year-old heads was quite simple yet very profound. People buy for their own reasons, not ours.

Once again, in the old days, traditional sales training talked mostly about things like persistence, not taking "no" for an answer, persuading customers to buy, and learning the best closing techniques. Much like an army storming the castle gates. While there are elements of each that are still vitally important, successful selling today should be much more sincere, more subtle, and more about helping the prospect buy from you by creating a compelling offer and tapping into latent desires rather than by trying to smash down the front door.

Probably more than anything else, in terms of ultimate selling success, is our ability to help match what we sell with what the customer needs and to make the transaction desirable in terms of positive outcomes. It is the continuation of the marketing process of creating "attractiveness" to our product or service. There are two ways to do that.

One, if you have the logical buyer, is to create tangible reasons why they should act. Business buyers will most commonly move forward if one or more of the following conditions exist, and there are three. *To save money. To increase profit. To improve efficiency.* If you cannot satisfy one or more of these requirements, then you are not likely going to make the sale and are much more likely to go home empty-handed.

Two, if you have an emotional buyer, their concerns are likely to revolve around status, experience, or comfort. This is much more likely a scenario in a consumer sale. Again, if you cannot show the prospect how he or she will attain the desired outcome for exchanging their hard-earned money for what you have, they will keep it stuffed tightly in their wallets.

Sales training has often stressed the ability to *persuade* the prospect into buying. That has too often simply been a nicer word for *manipulation.* And while you may be able to do it once, it is not a recipe for success in the long run, especially if you hope to have repeat customers. It is much more about having influence with your customer. Influence built on trust, reputation, authority, and expertise. It requires an earnest and skillful effort on your part to match up what you have to offer with what your potential customer is wishing to attain.

One of my favorite visuals for selling is that of the chameleon. It is us on the selling side of the table that have to be able to adjust ourselves. Buyers simply have too many choices today and are highly unlikely to put themselves in a situation where they exchange their money for something that they just don't feel good about buying. By embracing being a chameleon and creating the most favorable conditions for our customers, we give ourselves the best chance of earning their trust and comfort, which are crucial to making the sale.

Tom Sawyer made painting a fence seem so compelling, other kids insisted on picking up their brushes to finish the job. Being attractive, being flexible, creating desire, and delivering results equals lots of sales as well as happy customers.

> *"Social interaction is an 'enabler' and not a goal in itself."* ~ Jonathan Becher, CMO, SAP

Tom didn't engage his friends for the sake of talking with them. He ultimately wanted them to do the painting. The engagement or conversation was the enabler to getting them to paint the fence. It wasn't the goal itself.

*"Too many organizations fail to look beyond the sheer ease of access that social channels offer them and see the opportunities social offers for establishing relationships with current and potential customers."* ~ Josh Mait, CMO Relationship Science LLC and author for Inc.

Your online presence is just that. It is an enabler to the future sale. As the above quote mentions, it isn't just about posting anything on Facebook. Go beyond and you become your own Tom Sawyer. You build and tap into the relationships you have with your followers, becoming more attractive to them the more value you add.

Research your ideal clients as thoroughly as they research you. It is only then you can speak to their needs, understand their pain, and communicate in a way they understand, that they begin to trust you. Trust ultimately leads to the sale . . . or the whitewashed fence in Tom's case.

In the past, this might have been left to the marketing or advertising department, but today, you, as a sales professional, must understand your customer more than ever before. A potential customer may start following the company on Twitter or you as an employee.

Case in point . . . A company hires an outside resource to post on their social channels. The content is beautiful, but because it isn't personalized, it gets no traction. Posting isn't enough. To even be seen by their future customers, those individuals need to engage. What prompts someone to engage is their interest in the content. What inspires them to purchase is the company's ability to understand them speaking to them in their words.

When the company begins to understand their customer, they add more personalized posts. The engagement on their profile soars. Ultimately, they land new clients.

They may follow you as well.

If you share relevant content, they engage. If they engage, it doesn't mean they are ready to buy, just as Ben Rogers wasn't ready to whitewash the fence when he approached Tom, but after a conversation, not only was Ben ready to paint, but also hand over his apple!

Social selling is first and foremost social. It is about interacting and building relationships with people who have a desire for your product or service. It is getting to know them well enough that you understand how your product or service solves a problem for them, even if they haven't identified it. Like Tom, you will soon have your own following asking for your products and services.

## Set (Big) Goals

> *"A salesman is got to dream, boy. It comes with the territory"*
>
> ~Arthur Miller, *Death of a Salesman*

I've always been a bit over the top when it comes to setting goals. Probably listened to every goal-setting cassette (I miss the '80s) that was ever made. I admit it. I can be fiercely (and probably) annoyingly competitive at times. Just try to beat me in a game of Monopoly, or even Go Fish.

I had four big goals in my adult life: to get an MBA, to become VP Sales & Marketing, to earn a Black Belt, and to write a book. Check, check, check, and, check.

I say it with no ego (I hope). Instead, it was the obsessive, systematic pursuit of things that I passionately wanted to attain, and was willing to "pay the price" to achieve them.

Sales is, in my opinion, still and always will be one of the truest forms of self-expression in the world. As Walt Disney famously said, "If you can dream it, you can do it." Sales results, more than almost any other profession, are beholding to the effort that we are willing to invest to achieve them. We set our goals. We control our effort. And, while we can never control the outcome in any given situation, experience shows that much invested is almost always much rewarded.

At work, it goes without saying that we've attempted to create "stretch goals" where we are pushing ourselves to be the best we can be. Around the house, I always tried to instill in my kids the same sense of setting big goals. Last year when we went to the pumpkin patch to grab our fall jack-o'-lanterns, 9-year-old Annie said, "Daddy, I want to get the biggest pumpkin here." "I'll make you a deal," I said, "you can have the biggest pumpkin you can carry back and put on the scale." With a nod of her head, she was off.

One-half hour later, after scouring the entire pumpkin patch, here she comes, wobbly little legs bent under the crush of a 26-pound pumpkin which she proudly placed on the scale. And, I almost didn't mind paying $22 for a 26-pound pumpkin that we were about to plunge a knife into.

In all areas of life, including selling, big goals, properly and passionately pursued, create big results.

The best online selling efforts start with goals—big goals. Going back to our conversation about social media being an enabler, those goals may not look like traditional sales goals. Social goals may be about engagement, clicks, interactions, all of which build trust which then can lead to sales.

One of the first goals I recommend for sales teams is to understand the platforms they plan to use. This includes the how-tos, as well as the nature of the platform. What works? What does not? How do you build relationships on the platform? How do you turn people off? As uncomfortable as it may feel, to gain proficiency in social selling, you may have to go back to school.

The next goal I recommend is to identify the key performance indicators for your platform. What measurable activities tie directly to your sales goal? Generally, it isn't the number of fans on a page, but the engagement, demographics, and clicks back to the website that are more important indicators of future sales.

Now you can set intelligent, realistic, and timely social selling goals. Determine where you want to be in 6 months to a year. Write it down. Develop your action plan. Assess every day, week, month, quarter. Measure often. Adjust as needed.

Setting big goals is the first commitment. Looking at the future is the second. Third, you must commit to taking the steps necessary to put your plan into action.

*Did you know . . .*

> *61% of the most effective online content marketers discuss their strategies either daily or weekly and most have a written plan.* ~ Content Marketing Institute and Marketing Profs 2016 Benchmarks, Budgets and Trends for North America

# How to Earn an "A" in Selling

*"If you do not know how to ask the right question, you discover nothing"*

~ W. Edwards Deming

One of the greatest dangers for the new salesperson is the fear created by thinking you don't know enough and worried that you are not seen as competent if you have to ask questions. One of the greatest dangers for the experienced salesperson is the thought that you are so competent that you know it all and don't need to ask questions. Either way, the lack of not asking enough questions is the problem.

Asking more questions is the best way to earn an "A" grade in selling.

A business relationship differs from a strictly personal one in that there are some rules and expectations around the exchange of money for products and services. But, it is the same as a personal relationship in that you must know something of the person and their situation in order to be of any value. And the only way to do that is to ask questions.

Could you imagine (or maybe you have experienced) going on a date and the other person does nothing but talk all night . . . about themselves. All of the things they've done, places they've gone, and a hundred and one factoids about their life. You might suffer through the evening, but chances are great there won't be a second date.

In a selling situation, it is imperative that you ask questions to determine the right solutions for each individual prospect. No two opportunities, no matter how similar, are the same. Especially in today's ultrapersonalized world. Buyers expect—and demand—customization. That kind of specificity can only be created by, and come from, asking lots of questions.

Think about developing a "play sheet" with the 20 or so most common questions you need answered in order to better present your solution. You need not use them all every time, but you will be prepared for each opportunity to ask the right ones for that particular interaction.

In school, you may be happy with a B grade if you did your best. In selling and business development, a B grade may get you nothing but sent home . . . empty-handed.

What is it you are doing when you ask questions? You are inviting the other person into a conversation.

*Conversation* is defined as:

> *"The use of speech for informal exchange of views, ideas, or information, etc."*

Going back to its origin, according to vocabulary.com, the word *conversation* comes from the French word with the same spelling meaning "manner of conducting oneself in the world." To have a true conversation, one person shares information, the other listens intently and responds appropriately.

Why go into all the semantics about conversation?

Social selling is about asking questions, inviting conversation, and engaging the other person. It does not work if you shout at the other person or if you do all the talking. Instead, social selling depends on the art of engaging others in dialogue or written conversation.

Asking questions to engage potential customers online is a skill that takes practice. A great place to start is by listening online. In doing so, you learn what your potential customers are discussing.

Think about it this way: if you go to a party, do you barge right into a group discussion or do you listen? From there, you can respond either with a comment or question that is relevant. You employ the same technique online, but by engaging with a question, you ensure to garner the attention of the person speaking because they need to respond.

What type of question should you ask? You want to ask questions to better understand the other person's situation or position. In doing so, you can determine how best to serve.

# Turning Over Rocks and Finding Prospects

*"Top salespeople understand they must learn to feel comfortable doing the uncomfortable"*

~ Tim Sales

I admit it. I am a complete dinosaur. I grew up in the era of cold-calling. And, I don't mean just the telephone kind where you "dial for dollars." That is relatively easy. It is a more nonpersonal kind of rejection. No, I'm talking about the bona fide wear-out-your-shoes-door-to-door variety. Where you did not know anyone behind the door. You knocked, you entered (if they let you), and you tried to get through the gatekeeper and to someone in authority who had decision-making power for what you sold.

Scary stuff.

Believe it or not, I know, based on experience, that it can still work from time to time. We've actually opened up some customers in the last few years doing it. People still go to networking meetings, trade shows, and other events because, as social creatures, we still like *face-to-face* human interactions. But it is not, nor should it be, your primary way of prospecting in the twenty-first century. Sending out your sales force into the field is an expensive proposition. Turning over every stone, or trying to open every door, is an exceptionally ineffective way of finding and cultivating prospective customers for most sales organizations today.

Because of the Internet, buyers have the ability to find out about your company, your products, and services, and even about you, all without leaving the comfort of their office chair. But, it is a two-way street. You also have the ability to do your homework and find the most appropriate organizations and individuals to target without the need of trying to get your 10,000 steps in for the day.

If you are on the younger side, this comes as naturally to you as breathing. You were born and bred with your fingers attached to electronic devices. For those of us who grew up in or close to the baby boomer generation, this often is a wee bit less comfortable.

Learn all you can and become highly proficient at modern social media and other prospecting techniques. In all likelihood, in many selling situations, they need to be your primary weapon in your hunting process. But, you can still meet some interesting people that just may need what you have if you know how, and when, to knock on the right doors.

If you are a fan of America's Test Kitchen's and Cook's Country, you know Chris Kimball. Whether you like him or not isn't the point, it is what Chris is doing that is important.

Chris Kimball started the magazine *Cook's Illustrated* in 1993 with several unique premises. First, there would be no advertising, and it would feature tested recipes that were foolproof. This magazine spun off to the PBS show *America's Test Kitchen* in 2001 and *Cook's Country* in 2008.

In 2007, subscription to the magazine grew to 1 million with an additional 300,000 subscribers online. According to NPR, *America's Test Kitchen* has over 2 million viewers.

At the end of 2015, due to contract disputes, Chris left the enterprise.

Can you imagine walking away from everything you built? Oh, and what does this have to do with finding new prospects?

In the spring of 2016, Chris began a new venture, Milk Street Kitchen, in Boston. It is a departure from his *America's Test Kitchen* point of view, but includes a cooking school, magazine, and possible television show.

Chris had to start from scratch. Yes, he had a personal brand out there, but still, day one, zero subscribers, zero fans. What did Chris and his team do?

He is building community. In his own words in an e-mail from June 2016, *"So many of you have shown up to welcome us back, to support our efforts, to give us a chance to build a new community."*

Chris understands no one will buy his magazine, watch his show, or take a cooking class if he doesn't reach out. He knows he needs to build, and possibly rebuild, the trust people had in him from *Cook's Illustrated* to take a chance on him in the new adventure. He is sharing, using social tools such as e-mail, Facebook, Twitter, and Instagram, snippets of what is happening. Being a fan, I immediately jumped on board!

The communication has been sincere and heartfelt. It gives me a taste of what is to come. I'm already prepared to expect something different. All this is being done virtually. He doesn't have anything yet. He had no product, yet I became a prospect for what is to come just through his online presence.

The biggest shift a business can take is to look at their online efforts like Chris. It is to build a community where people want to find out about what is going on in your company and how they can engage. Community above all will uncover prospects ready to engage . . . and ultimately buy.

# How to Become a Sales ACE

*"The world is the great gymnasium where we come to make ourselves strong"*

~ Swami Vivekananda

Though there is some debate among experts as to the exact origins of the term "ace," its connotation is unmistakable. The title of ace was first used to celebrate the accomplishments of the aerial combat pilots in World War I. The designation conferred instant hero status on those "knights of the air."

Governments, eager to build support for the war at home, eagerly promoted the kills of those aces. Citizens in each country looked up to them for portraying persistence, talent, and courage. Competitive soldiers, driven by the desire for medals, fame, and fortune, eagerly accepted and embraced both the attention and the accolades.

While hopefully none of us are at war with the competition, top salespeople today should always strive to be "Red Barons" of the sales arena. Competitive salespeople, eager for acknowledgment, recognition, and rewards, need to go all-out to be an ACE in their careers.

## How to Become a Sales ACE

Here are three ways to be the modern-day sales version of Manfred von Richthofen or Eddie Rickenbacker. **A**ccelerate. **C**alculate. **E**levate.

*Accelerate.* Just as in aerial combat, the faster plane had an advantage; in sales, speed is a major weapon in modern sales warfare. Consider these two ways to accelerate your sales results.

Do more. In many instances, sales may not be quite as much of a numbers game as it once was, but it is still an activity game. In any area of sales (or life), you will almost never achieve your performance goals without hitting your activity goals. Just as the aces were judged by the number of downed enemy planes, salespeople will always be judged by the number of new accounts opened or total dollar value of their account assignment. In other words: results. To create the optimum number of qualified opportunities, it may still take more calls, going to more events, setting more appointments, etc., to judge when you have enough of the very best of what you are looking for. More opportunities will always give you more chances to win exactly the battles you want to win. Hustle, properly directed, solves a lot of problems.

But have less. To move faster, sometimes you have to carry fewer things. In sales, if we have too many prospects or the wrong customers, it can actually slow us down. Constantly, evaluate both prospects and customers and decide if they are an ideal fit for you and your organization. Be both ruthless and quick to dispatch those opportunities that simply don't fit. Engaging in more opportunities than you or your organization can handle or don't really want will ultimately result in fewer sales. By saying yes to everything, the reality is that you are not prioritizing well enough. The best answer is to treat the right prospects and customers with more A-level attention rather than too many prospects with only a B-level effort. Say no to questionable opportunities. Fire troublesome customers. You may be surprised at how focusing on the right things will really equal more speed—and—results.

*Communication.* The World War I aces often challenged the enemy only when the odds were substantially in their favor. Communication, even in the preradar, pre-Internet age relied on messaging that put pilots in a more favorable position to engage and win the conflicts that they were faced with. In the movie *The American President*, President Andrew Shepherd (Michael Douglas) made the comment that, "We fight the fights that are worth fighting, and we fight the fights we can win." Here are two ways that being a better communicator helps salespeople win the battle and leads to greater sales success.

Internal. Salespeople have often (justifiably) been criticized for thinking every first meeting is going to turn into the next "big one." They run back to the office and get everyone scrambling around to satisfy the "hot" prospect. All too often, only later, after much effort, does everyone really find out that they were not so hot after all. Most B2B sales organizations now rely on multidisciplinary teams to deliver customer solutions. The sales rep, if he or she is the communication quarterback for the internal team, must not say that they can win every battle. That will exhaust resources, and they will end up losing credibility in the process.

External. In much the same way as an increase in internal team members, it is now not uncommon for external decision-making teams to include three, four, or more people. Sales cycles get extended through more complicated evaluation and review processes. This exponentially increases the challenge for salespeople to stay in communication with all members of the prospect's team. It becomes critical to stay on top of voice mails, e-mails, texts, and all other forms of communication so as to not miss anything that might leave a bad impression . . . or even worse, sink the deal.

*Elevate.* In aerial combat, the aircraft at the higher altitude always had the advantage. To achieve ultimate success in selling, elevation is also mission-critical. Try these two ways to gain greater heights in your sales career.

Start at the Top. The fastest way to climb the mountain is to begin at the top. In the book *Summiting*, by Jim Hoverman, he states that "Your ability to consistently have 'value conversations' with top management influencers is a skill that is no longer a 'nice-to-have' but, in reality, a '*got-to-have.*'" Any salesperson that has begun a relationship with a new customer knows the difference in having the support of the company executives versus only lower-level employees. While these conversations are not probable if you are only providing a commodity product or service, if your proposition has measurable return on investment, C-level people will almost always take notice and be involved in the decision-making process.

Constantly raise your skills. In today's hypercompetitive business environment, there is no room for standing still. You must get better today than you were yesterday. And better tomorrow than you were today as well. Learn all you can about time management. Get and stay up with everything to do with social media. Commit to lifelong learning when it comes to nutrition and fitness, healthy living, and continually increasing your sales skills.

The ace pilots of long ago were totally committed to acceleration, communication, and elevation to win the dogfights they engaged in. Modern-day sales ACE's often win their current-day battles with the competition in just the same way.

Besides being a sales ACE on the ground, are you an ACE in the virtual world? If you are an ACE in the field, you must be an ACE online, but what does that look like?

**Accelerate**—You must accelerate your authentic presence on your social channels. This does not mean just posting more stuff, but instead, showing up and engaging. A recent conversation with friends illustrated the importance of acceleration online.

They recently restarted their business after a couple years of taking a corporate job because they realized they were an entrepreneur at heart. They knew the important part their social networks would plan in the ramp-up. Part of their strategy was to spend time, both morning and evening, engaging on the two platforms where they felt most comfortable and where, they determined, their ideal clients resided.

Within 6 months, their business was up and running in a big way with clients in several states. They attributed the success to consistently showing up to their community.

Note how this also speaks to the slowing down as well. They didn't jump on all the platforms. They strategically chose the platforms where they knew they would see results. By concentrating their efforts, they achieved larger results.

**Communicate**—Learning how to use customer-centric communication on social channels is the next component of being an ACE salesperson online.

If you were to go onto your social channels right now, notice which people, brands, or companies you consistently stop or hover over to learn more. Are there certain newsletters you consistently open? Ask yourself why.

In doing so, you will uncover the secrets of a Communication ACE. I'll bet you feel as though they are speaking to you, right? The information they share is on target and useful. You feel as though they have put effort into their articles rather than just written something to meet a deadline.

When you engage them online, they are authentic, helpful, and engaged. They don't assume because you have a question you are ready to buy, another sign you are dealing with a Communication ACE.

Now, look at your own online efforts. If they don't match up, take a lesson from the ACE.

**Elevate**—In the online world, things change weekly. It is important you elevate your knowledge of how the platforms work and you accept new changes rather than bemoaning the updates.

Why is this important?

By embracing the ever-changing social world, you stay on top of it. When there is something new, you are eager to learn about it and use it. This act alone will elevate your game on your social network.

Another way to elevate your actions is through the people you follow. Can you follow more influential people in your industry or in the prospective companies you want to work with? It is great to gather followers who are interested with your information. They can be potential customers and clients. But, when you actively seek out those higher-level influencers, you begin to engage at a much-different level.

Becoming an online ACE may feel daunting. It is. No one becomes an ACE just by wishing it would happen. You have to have skin in the game to make it work. What steps can you take in the next month to raise yourself to ACE level?

# How Are You Different?

*"Why fit in when you were born to STAND OUT?"*
~ Dr. Seuss

According to the Food Marketing Institute, last year, the average grocery store in the United States carried 42,214 unique items. Dozens of brands of cereal, potato chips, candy, and cans of soup. Look around at the explosion of consumer choices and it becomes mind-numbingly overwhelming. It extends to B2B sales as well. In a sea of ever-increasing competitors and products with similar features or benefits, how do you stand out?

Certainly in the marketing arena the goal is to help identify and promote the differences of your product or service from that of your competitor. But, if your advertisements, claims, or results are similar to those of your competitors, it is up to your salespeople to show the prospect the positive differences of your organization over that of the others that they are considering.

If your salespeople cannot show how you are different, your chances of making the sale goes down dramatically. As an individual, perhaps the biggest weapon you have is you. People like authenticity in both personal and business situations. Being you is always being different than someone else in another company, store, or service.

In the transaction, differential selling includes three things: usage, value, and price.

*Usage and value.* Does your product go faster or last longer? Does it come in more colors or can it be customized? Does it hold more or is it environmentally friendly and "green"? Do you have better customer testimonials and levels of user satisfaction? If so, how successfully can you share the information and tap into the unique reasons that will make a positive difference to each prospective customer?

*Price.* Does it cost less? Why? And why should the customer care? Does it cost more? Same questions. If there is not a big difference in price, can you provide good reasons why the extra $.05, $5, or $500 is worth the difference. Sometimes helping show buyers that they are not *spending* $1,000 with you, that they are *only* spending $100 more with you than with someone else, makes all the difference in how they *feel* about buying something.

The demand for personalized marketing communication and social media research when evaluating purchasing something will likely only continue to increase. Despite that, buying decisions still often come down to a salesperson's ability to help explain the differences between what you have to offer and what the competition has to offer.

Spend plenty of time making sure you know how to share the right information at the right time.

"Stories are how we learn best. We absorb numbers, facts and details, but we keep them all glued into our heads with stories." ~ Chris Brogan

The fourth component of differential selling, especially when it comes to digital selling, is being able to tell your story.

Your story is what surrounds usage, value, price, and demand. It builds context for your potential customer. It helps them get to know, like, and trust you. It also lets them know how you relate to them. Because online selling is 24/7, the focus of your interactions and engagement is about consistently telling your story.

*"Stop interrupting what people are interested in, and be what people are interested in."* ~ Mike Schoultz

Think of the best storytellers you know. What about their stories engage you? What about the stories draws you in? The best stories allow you to become involved emotionally because you connect to the hero's situation.

Now, let's think about what we consider the sales process of extoling the virtues of the features and benefits of your product or services. Does this tell a story? Does this engage you or draw you in? Probably not.

Now, let's look at an example from Guinness brought to my attention in a Mike Schoultz blog.

The ad shows a woman bartender placing a Guinness on an empty table night after night. She cleans the table, and silently let's people know not to sit there. Enter a returning soldier. She smiles and nods toward the table and the waiting Guinness. As the patrons in the bar raise a silent glass to the soldier, the voice-over says, "The choices we make reveal the true nature of our character." I dare you not to get teary-eyed watching the video (https://www.youtube.com/watch?v=TnldM0nNZ0w).

Guinness didn't rant and rave about their beer. They linked the experience of the beer, their beer in the bar, with a bigger message. Your choices reveal your nature. Most people believe they would act similarly to the bartender. They can relate to her. She becomes the hero of the story, and so do you as the watcher if you identify with her. Guinness just becomes one of those high-quality choices you make, especially in situations like this.

Notice neither the beer nor the company are the hero. When you think about the story you want to tell online, it must be relatable in all the best senses to the highest qualities your potential customer wants for themselves and their company. When you link that indirectly to your product, your potential customer gets the message and is more inclined to feel positive toward your company, brand, products, and you, the salesperson.

You can share your story in video, as Guinness did, or you can tell your story with images on Instagram the way Anthropologie does in showing the lifestyle of their hero. You won't find staged fashion shoots on Anthropologie's Instagram. Instead, you might find two models playing with a puppy, eating ice cream, or on comfy bed in a cabin. The images tell the story of a day in the life of their potential customers.

Your passions, your purpose, your focus are part of your story. Uncover these and you will find your unique voice that resonates with your perfect customer or client.

# Don't Get Stuck in the Potholes of the Past

*"Hardships often prepare ordinary people for an extraordinary destiny . . ."*

~ C. S. Lewis

Emotionally, we humans can be very funny. We sometimes spend more time and energy looking backward than looking forward. We beat up ourselves (or others) for the things that went wrong, did not happen, or that we have regrets over.

In my experience, selling is one of the most prevalent professions for this to happen. It is often a "zero sum" game. Win the order and you're happy. Lose the order and, well . . . There usually is no prize for second place. I've seen numerous good salespeople get stuck looking at where things went wrong, the car went off the road and got stuck in a proverbial pothole, never to climb out and get to the finish line in first place. And, they let it drag them down.

In baseball, they often talk about the need to have a "closer's mentality." It is not a job for the faint of heart. You may win (close) a few games in a row, and then . . . *bam!* One night a closer might give up a home run to lose the game. But, they need to have a very short memory because chances are, they will be right back out there on the mound again tomorrow night.

And so it is with sales. We lose a sale or two and our emotions can go haywire. Down in the dumps. Loss of confidence. There is only one recipe to fix it. Forget about it.

If, after any unsuccessful sales call/proposal we could remember that there are four specific things to review—and then move on—we would be better off.

1. What went wrong? It *is* important to figure that out. It is also important *not* to dwell on it and become stuck. Go get the next one.
2. What would I have done differently? If you've taken the time to understand what didn't work, then, hopefully, you've come up with a list of options of what might have worked, and that you'll try those with the next similar opportunity.
3. Can we "stay in touch" for future opportunities? Using the baseball analogy again, it is OK to keep yourself "on deck." There may be another chance to get up to bat soon.
4. Did I get a referral? Even in a no scenario, there may be someone in the prospect's organization or circle of friends who may also consider your offering.

In my sales manager days when reps would head out into the field, my standard line was "Don't come home empty-handed." If you can remember these four things, even if you don't win the sale, you will come home with both important lessons and with something of value for the future.

*"The modern consumer is digitally driven, connected & mobile empowered. Sales reps need to adapt or be replaced."* ~ Jill Rowley

Now, let's layer in social selling. With changing algorithms, enhancements, and new platforms, selling in the digital world is fraught with potholes beyond merely losing the sale. Strategies, if not monitored, may easily become antiquated overnight, resulting in wasted time and money.

First, let's quantify if social selling is even worth the effort. Here are some statistics compiled by Sales For Life:

- 72.6 percent of salespeople who used social selling as part of their sales process outperformed their peers.
- Salespeople using social selling exceeded quota 23 percent more often than those who don't.

The biggest pothole is that the buying process is changing faster than organizations are responding to it, according to 69 percent of sales managers. If social selling is worth it, how can you avoid its potholes?

Here are three ways to avoid digital potholes:

1. Allocate time monthly to stay educated on the platforms you use. Understand trends, updates, etc. This can be taking regular Webinar, live classes, watching product updates, or by reading online articles.

   Places to get started are colleges, chambers of commerce, SCORE, or the Small Business Association. You could also start a mastermind group within your organization and meet on a regular basis with the focus on learning more about social. Even . . . bring in an expert.

2. Only trust information from credible sources. There is a lot of hearsay with social platforms; in order to get the best

information, vet your sources. Trusting what others say on Facebook about Facebook may lead you into more of a ditch than a pothole. Finding credible sources such as the platform blog, industry journals, or even vetted sources will save you time and energy and keep you on the paved surface.

3. Measure your results, track your efforts, and adjust. This is the best way to understand first, if changes are affecting your efforts, and second, to adjust to avoid months of lost time and money. Sales is always about being nimble. Put those practices to work on a regular basis to reap the rewards.

You have a choice. You can hit a pothole and remain there—or, you can look at your pothole as an opportunity to learn and grow. Capitalizing on the next update to Facebook, Instagram, Snapchat, or Periscope can give you a competitive advantage. You decide.

# Take the "Plunge" for More Sales

> *"Go confidently in the direction of your dreams! Live the life you've imagined"*
>
> ~ Henry David Thoreau

So there I found myself at high noon on January 1st, standing alongside about 250 of my friends and neighbors ready to participate in the annual Penguin Plunge, eager to hurl ourselves down the beach and into the Atlantic Ocean to kick off the start of a new year, and apparently, the swimming season.

It occurred to me that there were three pretty good sales lessons to be learned that day. Having a hot chocolate stand there could have been number four, but we'll save that one for now.

Here's what I figured out:

1. You have to learn about it before you can buy (do) it. The person I was standing next to on the beach said to me, "I never knew they did this every year. I just happened to see the sign by chance the other day and had to come try it." In building a successful sales system, you must first engage in marketing

communications to make potential customers aware of and excited about your product, service, or event. No awareness, no customers.

2. Somebody has to go in first. When penguins dive in the water to catch their food, there is always a first one to go off the beach or the iceberg to notice if there are any potential predators around. Banish any kind of call reluctance. Memo to self: there will *always* be predators (i.e., *competitors*)—dive in first anyway and make sure you get to eat instead of being eaten.
3. There is power in numbers. Somehow, I know that if each of the people on the beach that day had to go one at a time, fewer people would have reached the water. But you simply could not deny yourself the experience of running down the beach en masse. There is an energy and enthusiasm that comes from achieving goals with others. Engage all the members of your team in accomplishing your big goals.

Good reminders for selling and I'll reread this when I wonder next year why I'm standing on the beach again.

Tackling social selling may feel as foreign or chilly as taking the Penguin Plunge. You may even have said, "I'll never use social selling. I have a system that works. This digital stuff won't work in my environment."

The truth is . . . Digital is here. Social selling certainly is not the only way to sell to your customer, but it is a viable channel and needs to be explored, as foreign as that may seem. Today, you are lucky to have multiple resources not available 5 years ago, to learn to use the social tools, how to measure success, and how to enhance your chances of selling using social.

It might feel safer to wait until you understand it all or have a perfect plan in place. That would be great, but things move fast out there. As soon as you get everything perfect, things can change. Then your "perfect" is not perfect any more.

Look at how the platforms and even our smart phones evolve. Facebook or Apple isn't sitting there waiting until they can include all the features they want to add to their products. Instead, they organize what is most needed or requested. They get to work on those, and when they are ready, they launch. They add updates as they go along.

Take a lesson from their actions. Jump in. Get started. Whether it is using a new platform, starting a blog, or sending your first e-newsletter, you must launch to get started.

Seth Godin sums it up in these two quotes:

> *"Perfection is an illusion."*
>
> *"The only purpose of starting is to finish, and while projects we do are never really finished, they must ship."*

You may be hindered in your organization because of traditional thinking or in your industry because of regulations or even in your own head because of fear. I get it. I've been there.

Don't use these as an excuse not to jump in, however. When you do, you are falling farther behind. Instead, tap into your inner resolve to excel and get in the game.

Diving into social may feel as frigid as taking the Penguin Plunge, but at least you can do it from the warmth of your office.

# Don't Shoot Yourself in the Foot

*"Dontopedalogy is the science of opening your mouth and putting your foot in it"*

~ Prince Philip

People buy from people they like and trust. Likeability and trust are frequently created on seemingly inconsequential but critical communication and relationship skills.

There are five things that you need to avoid that are almost guaranteed to turn prospects off and have your feet walking out the door and some other salesperson's feet walking in.

1. Acting smarter than the prospect. Salespeople who try to be the smartest person in the room don't impress anyone. Of course, those who present that way will deny that they would ever act like that deliberately. But when they nod their heads impatiently while a prospect talks or drums their fingers on a table, they send a message that they don't want to hear what's being said.
2. Passing judgment. There's nothing wrong with offering an opinion during a presentation. But it's not a good idea to pass

judgment about what a prospect is saying. Try to accept ideas as they are presented with complete neutrality. By not expressing negative opinions initially, you can reduce the number of pointless arguments that go nowhere and often result in not making the sale.

3. Starting a sentence with "no," "but," or "however." When a salesperson starts a sentence with any of these words, no matter how friendly the tone, the message to the prospect is, "You're wrong."
4. Making destructive comments. These are the thoughtless remarks that run the gamut from jabs at competitors to unkind remarks about former customers. A good way to cure this habit is to ask yourself whether the comment will help your customers, your company, or the person you're talking to.
5. Passing the buck. A salesperson who can't shoulder the blame is not someone who builds long-term relationships with customers. While they're trying to save their own skin, they just end up sending a negative message to their customers.

If you engage in any of these mistakes, it can ultimately be the worst kind of sales prevention for your business. Often, it is not the big things or even the price of your product or service that wins or loses the sale. Very often, it is the little things that simply don't "feel right" to the buyer and turns them off.

Building trust is the cornerstone of social selling. To build trust, you must take these five statements to the next level because it is easy to act smarter, pass judgement, passively say they are wrong, make destructive comments, and pass the buck online.

Why?

Because for many, being online is safe. It is like the person in a retail store that stays behind the counter. The computer screen, like the counter, provides a false sense of security. It is easy to feel smarter or pass judgement on the other person when you have the screen between them. Customers, perhaps even *your* customers, have told me they won't do business with a company because of what a salesperson, or even the owner, said or posted online. Instead, they silently withdraw their purchases, sponsorships, and/or donations. The most difficult thing for the organization is they can't pinpoint this type of behavior unless it is dramatic.

Those that succeed at social selling regard the computer as a portal to the other person's world rather than a shield. They engage. They ask questions. They genuinely and authentically relate to the other person, even if it is through words on a screen. They regard the social space as if they are being interviewed by a national publication. They understand there are potentially thousands of people watching, so they, in turn, treat the platform with respect.

Because they authentically represent themselves, when you meet them in person, you are not surprised. In fact, the relationship that may have started with a LinkedIn or Twitter conversation continues.

Authentically representing yourself means that you are the same online and off-line. It means you aren't writing one thing to "hook" your prospect, and then doing another. It means you aren't bad-mouthing your connections and customers off-line because you know they are the link to future sales. You value your online relationships. There is no difference between meeting someone online and in person.

When you make that transition and begin treating your online connections with respect, they soon not only will become prospects and customers, but they will become a powerful online sales force.

# Selling Lessons of the Changing Seasons

*"We cannot become what we want by remaining what we are"*

~ Max De Pree

There is a time for every season and every purpose under the sun I've heard it was written. At the time of this writing, we are moving from summer and into autumn in New England. A beautiful time of year with an explosion of colors and the need to break out the sweaters to handle the cooler weather. Nature adapts seamlessly to change. It takes people a little more time and effort. Being able to adapt to changing circumstances is essential in any job or career. None more so than sales.

In thinking about the two seasons we are adapting to right now, eight lessons come to mind.

In summer and at other times of the year like the holidays, we tend to slow down and take it easy. While I'm not advocating all work and no play, speeding up when others are slowing down or not trying as hard is a great way to get ahead of the competition.

While in many industries there is a normal slowing of business due to increased time off, it does not mean that you can't maintain peak performance in the summer, during the holidays, or any other traditionally slow times.

At those times of the year, consider these thoughts:

1. Make more calls. Yes, I said *more*. Yes, you are likely to miss more people because they are away. But your message will stand out when they get it because so many fewer salespeople are leaving them at this time.
2. Stop by more places. With more people on vacation, that means that the "gatekeepers" just may be away as well. It might mean you'll get easier access to the person you really want to see.
3. Create more proposals. If there are people buying, go get them now while the competition isn't even trying. If you're in a business that can make special offers, do some now and lock up the business. If it is a slower time for you, this will help to keep your incoming orders flowing.
4. Organize yourself. Clean up your To-Do list. Get rid of old e-mails and things that you're never going to work on. Create a laser-sharp focus on what you want to be doing. If there are fewer people to see, work on yourself. Getting more organized in the short term means being more productive in the long run.

For other times of the year when things are more normal (if there is such a thing), consider these sales lessons from the fall:

1. Look for low-hanging fruit. On our recent trip to the apple orchard, I spent a good bit of time maneuvering the "picker" to reach high up into the trees to grab the apples at the top. But as we went along, I also grabbed some of the apples on the lower branches, and, even some on the ground. If you're looking to

make some deals, go for some of the ones on top but don't overlook the easy ones right there for the taking.

2. Embrace change. Change is in the air. The temperature. The amount of daylight. The color of the leaves. If you're like one of the now 7 billion people living on the planet, I'm guessing that you're experiencing some kind of change right now. Maybe it's because of technology, the economy, trends, styles, etc., or whatever. Don't fight it. Embrace it. Figure out how to profit, be healthier, and more productive because of it.
3. Look for extra time. We're about to turn back the clocks. That means we get one extra hour of time. In your busy schedule, look for some things you can drop (turn back) so that you can pick up a little extra time for the priorities in life.
4. Ask for the order. My kids didn't walk up to the doors on Halloween night, ring the bell, and say, "Would you like to think it over about giving me some candy?" No! They rang the bell or knocked on the door, it opened, and they said, "Trick or Treat!" And they came home with hundreds of orders . . . ah, I mean pieces of candy.

There are lessons for every season. Make sure you figure out some of your own for success at every time of the year.

I have always said the slow season is the best time to build your network and future customers. Instead of taking it easy, it is a time to dig deeper into your current database, make new connections, and listen more to uncover future needs of your existing customers. Then when you get to your busy season, you've got a new group of customers to serve.

Social selling is 24/7. Your digital footprint is always working for you, but during your slow season, it is a good time to review what has worked for you, consider what you need to alter, or perhaps reflect on what tools you want to use for the future. It is also a good time to reconnect with fans, followers, and friends. For example, when was the last time you spent time with your LinkedIn connections? Do you even know who you are connected to and why you are connected to them? Do you know who has recently joined LinkedIn that you know and aren't connected to yet?

The seasonality of your business can also allow for you to go back to those pending requests that get pushed off during the busy time and touch base. Sometimes the most unexpected sales can happen from a rekindled conversation.

Finally, slower times or changes in the season offer opportunities to actively listen online. You may be able to determine what new digital channels your prospects are using, who the influencers are in companies you want to do business with in the future, or what new questions your prospects are asking. You can also listen to what your competitors are talking about, how they are using social, and what types of content they are sharing. Once you get the hang of it, this is something you can add to your daily workflow.

Use the ebbs and flows of business to your advantage. Be there when your competition isn't. Engage when others are on vacation. Be of service when others are otherwise occupied. Whether you use digital or traditional means, don't let these opportunities slip by.

# How to Open Locked Doors

*"Continuous effort, not strength or intelligence, is the key to unlocking our potential"*

~ Winston Churchill

I sat down with my kids the other night and watched the newer version of the classic Roald Dahl story, *Charlie and the Chocolate Factory*. For the record, I'm a much-bigger fan of the original with Gene Wilder in the title role of Willy Wonka. That said, there was one particularly hilarious scene in the new version where Johnny Depp, as Willy Wonka, is fiddling with a large set of keys on his belt in an attempt to unlock a gate and let a frantic Mr. Salt get to Veruca in time before the super-trained, nut-opening squirrels do. One key after another is put in the lock and tried with no success until finally, Mr. Wonka finds the key that opens the gate. Unfortunately for Veruca and Mr. Salt, the open gate comes too late and they find themselves "down the garbage shoot." The squirrels had decided that they were bad nuts.

How many sales and how many dollars have you missed out on by not having the right key(s), only to find the potential business has "gone down the garbage shoot"?

## How to Open Locked Doors

We all wish that we could find the magic key or a skeleton key that would open every lock. But, the reality is that it is often a series of keys that opens a series of doors that eventually unlocks the sale and closes the deal in the end. Starting strong, having a plan, and being "pleasantly, professionally persistent" go a long way to making good things happen in the end.

Setting the right expectations right away is critical. First impressions really do count . . . a lot. Let your prospects know you're competent and trustworthy. This extends backward to everything that might be your prospect's initial contact: Web site, storefront, literature, ads, referrals, social media presence, etc. And, very importantly, your first conversation. A 1 percent variance in understanding may not seem like a big deal at the beginning, but if not addressed immediately, later on down the road, the gap between what you can do for your prospects and what they *think* you can do for them may be too large to overcome.

Most importantly, don't know too much. In the modern world, content is king. We spend many hours and many dollars fine-tuning our message and deciding how to deliver it to our prospects. But, just how much of it is what they are looking for?

Tony Robbins once said, "Successful people ask better questions and as a result, they get better answers."

Newer sales reps often are too nervous to ask enough questions because they feel that the prospect will think that they offer no value if they don't know all the answers. Veteran sales reps often don't ask enough questions because they feel that if they've been around for a while that they know all the answers. Both approaches are wrong—always.

Other times, armed with an increasingly overwhelming amount of features and benefits, sometimes we rush into a situation and tell the prospect all about what we have before asking what they, the potential customer, is really looking for. The ultimate cart-before-the-horse thinking, believing that we have the answers *before* we ask the questions. The best salespeople are detectives. They look around. They assess the situation. They don't come with all the answers right away. They don't know too much. They ask more and better questions.

Developing a repetitive process that includes a structured method of investigation works best. One of my favorite activities growing up was a good connect-the-dots book. It never failed to excite me to watch the picture of a butterfly or horse or cartoon character comes into focus as you went from number 1 to 2 to 3, etc. When I improvised and went out of order, the picture didn't come out too clearly. Doing things in the right order worked best to get the right result.

In sales, it is exactly like connect-the-dots. Too frequently, salespeople don't develop the discipline to ask the right questions and do the right things in the right order. The expression "flying by the seat of your pants" probably came about to describe the activity of some unsuccessful salesperson. With a little effort, if you study your opportunities, both wins and losses, you'll likely notice that some patterns will emerge. The victories will likely have a similar sequence of events that preceded the order or winning the business.

That does not mean becoming an inflexible slave to a rigid, unbending routine. Rather, you must realize that questions come before presentations, presentations come before asking for the order, and you must figure out where plant visits, free samples, white papers, or a seminar invitation fit to create the best sales process for your business.

Learning how to set expectations, ask more and better questions, and connecting-the-dots in your sales process will help you make sure the picture comes out right, and then more doors will be opened in the end.

In the digital world, there are probably more dots to connect than you have time to trace. You start the picture by asking questions about your customers and to your customers. YOU become a sponge. You learn as much as you can.

Then you move into the digital space and begin collecting data, more dots. Just like the connect-the-dots pictures; however, at some point, you are standing in the middle of a bunch of dots that make no sense, and you can't find the next number.

To find your way in the maze is to understand your key performance indicators (KPI). What are the numbers that mean the most to your sales effort? Once you determine your social KPIs, then you need to understand how to drive them.

The challenge here is there are metrics that make us feel good, like more people liking or connecting to us, but they are not always the best indicators. Instead, look at how many times people visit your page, share your information, or even where they come from, and *that* can lead you to more relationships and qualified prospects.

So what are quality sales metrics for social?

1. Number of e-mail list subscribers. When collected appropriately, meaning the person gave you permission to e-mail them, they have already raised their hand as interested in further communication with you. Companies focused on growing an engaged e-mail list, then using it to nurture and grow their prospects, find more success.

   The other reason this is a good key performance indicator is you own the list. Facebook or Twitter could go away tomorrow, but you own your list. Building a quality list is one of the biggest success factors for most businesses today.

2. Effectiveness of calls to action. It is easy to develop content and engage on social to increase your reach, but that doesn't always lead to conversion. To track sales effectiveness, you

must be able to track the activity generated around calls to action, be they small or large commitments. You do this by measuring the effectiveness of your calls to action.

To be effective, a call to action needs to inspire the reader or recipient to take the action you suggest. This can be influenced by relevance of the information offered, wording of the offer, placement of the call to action, etc. Understanding what works for your audience, and then using that information for future campaigns, will lead to sales.

3. Engagement of followers. Are the people following you reacting to your information, or is it passing them by? Are they clicking on your e-mail offer or deleting it? Are people sharing your information? These actions show the commitment of your fans or followers to your information and ultimately, your brand.

   As their engagement increases, so does your credibility. As your credibility increases, so does trust, and we all know when trust increases, so do sales.

# The Power of Celebration

*"Life should not only be lived, it should be celebrated"*

~ Ohso

It would not have been my first choice. But on their insistence, I braved the streets of Boston with three of my boys to go watch the Patriot's most recent Super Bowl victory rolling rally on the tops of the town's Duck Boats.

The improbable victory, after almost being foiled again by a miraculous catch, had brought out (and wrung out) a tidal wave of emotions with the team's fan base.

My older boy had been very convincing (salesperson in training?) and told me how this was a "once-in-a-lifetime" chance . . . despite the fact that there have been nine parades in Boston in the last 13 years. And while the crowd was more than a little, shall we say, "spirited," and that we waited for 2 hours in a snowbank so we could have a front-row view, I would not have traded the experience and memory.

After the economic downturn in 2008, I feel that many businesses lost something. In the obsessive cost-cutting and austerity philosophy that followed, I noticed that people did not celebrate their business victories in the same way, or in some cases, not at all.

I was always taught that in sales, you should celebrate your wins. Not just the big ones but the little victories along the way that were the building blocks that inevitably led to the larger ones. It was the way to keep your motivation up in the face of rejection and all of the effort it took to close even one deal.

Celebrating new customers, making your quota for a month as an office, even achieving a project goal like hitting the prescribed amount of phone calls or appointments were important tools in keeping everyone's spirits up. And keeping the momentum going. Without these types of celebrations, in my humble opinion, you might just keep up the wrong kind of momentum . . . going in the wrong direction.

But, with the added pressure that came with a less-than-robust economy, I saw companies "hunker down" quite a bit and pass on, or avoid, these kinds of celebrations. I think that is a bad mistake. People need to feel good and be recognized about their efforts and accomplishments. Nothing kills performance and hard work faster than being taken for granted.

For high-achieving individuals (and companies), it is critical to keep score. And what's the point of keeping score if you're not going to throw yourself a little party now and then when you accomplish something meaningful? It's one of the most important elements of human nature and one that was on display fully in both the fans and players at the victory parade.

Allow yourself and your organization some victory laps when you hit the mark on some important goals. It doesn't have to be a parade down the center of town, but it has to be something. A lunch, a bonus, a trip, a day off, even a thank-you note to someone. See if by incorporating a few more celebrations into your life, you can increase your level of performance. Build momentum in a positive direction. Winning never gets tired. And neither do the parades that celebrate it.

Celebrating successes makes us feel good, but also reinforces the right behaviors.

Frequently, I will see a spirited person in an organization embrace social selling. They try to engage their peers or even upper management with little to no effect. They work hard. They take their learning seriously. But, when they achieve great results, they get little to no accolades.

Three things can happen as a result. First, your excited budding social media explorer will give up. They quiet down and conform to the norm. They stop taking the initiative to innovate for the sake of the company. Is that what you want? Do you want your sales team and employees to be robots, just meeting expectations, or do you want them to exceed expectations?

The second, and more frequent thing that happens, is they leave your organization for one that is more progressive. Companies are increasingly losing talent because they choose to stick with what has always worked. Then they wonder why retention is low and sales are down.

Finally, potential customers will look elsewhere. If they were engaged by the initial efforts, but those stop, you lose their attention. When it comes time to buy, they go with a competitor because they forgot about you. I have also heard from salespeople who have let their online activity lapse is they find out later they lost a sale because when the consumer was doing their research, they didn't look credible enough online.

Celebrating success allows you to validate innovative thinking. It reinforces what they are doing as something of value to the company. I suggest you look at your sales team. Notice what they are doing and how they are achieving results. Celebrate not only the traditional sales systems but recognize and celebrate those who may be choosing to do something a little different. This could be a future sales avenue you never expected.

# Closing Is a Series of Small Commitments

> *"It's the little choices every day that lead to the final results we are striving for"*
>
> ~ Jason Bartels

I've often used this exercise in sales training classes. I'll ask someone to stand up, walk over to an open door, close it, then go sit down. After the task is accomplished, I ask the participants when the door closed. Almost always, they answer "when the door shut." I always respond that it started when I picked the volunteer and asked them to close it. And that there were a series of things that had to happen—making a request, standing, walking, actively closely the door, returning to their seat—that needed to occur to complete the task.

In the same way, there is a *moment* when a sale closes. It could be a handshake, the purchase order received, the verbal commitment, the contract signed, or certainly when the check is cashed. But ultimately, it is almost always built upon a series of activities and small commitments along the way that lead to achieving it. That is the nature of a sales cycle; discovery, investigation, evaluation, presentations, obtaining a yes or no.

Persistence is necessary for closing deals. Patient persistence is even better. Allowing the prospect the space to increase their comfort, trust, and confidence gradually is almost always better than trying to achieve it immediately.

It is a lot like dating. If we are looking for a relationship, it is very difficult to establish on the first date. It is a step toward building commitment. There are likely to be picnics, movies, dinners, giving gifts, meeting potential in-laws, and many other steps before the deal is closed.

If we can keep our prospect moving forward through a natural series of smaller steps, we have a better chance of closing the deal at the right time. Getting the first appointment, sending the literature, getting connected on LinkedIn, gaining acceptance for the demo or the plant visit, and gaining agreement to give a proposal are some of the logical steps in most sales processes.

Unless you're looking for a mail-order spouse, become a master at managing the smaller building blocks that lead to stronger, long-term relationships. And more sales.

Closing the deal includes how you interact with your potential customers online as well. Frequently, the first step in the sales process will happen online when someone reaches out with a question, comments on an article, or even starts to follow your social channels.

None of these actions are cause to bombard them with e-mails and sales literature. It is, however, a time for patience and persistence.

Let's look at an example of the process when it doesn't work.

I was looking for new ways to surprise and delight my customers. I found a website that offered unique items and an online catalogue to download. I completed the short form with my e-mail and phone and promptly received the catalogue.

The items were in line with what I was looking for and within budget. I was thrilled. I saved the catalogue to reference for the future.

It wasn't 24 hours later when I receive the expected e-mail asking how I liked the catalogue from a sales representative. They asked if I would like to follow up by phone. I replied not now but thank you, then deleted the e-mail because I was not ready to purchase yet.

The following day, I received not only an e-mail but a phone call asking, again, if I wanted to talk with someone. Again, I replied not now. I ignored the phone call, thinking the e-mail should be enough. That same day, I received another phone call from a different salesperson in the organization. Apparently, the e-mail wasn't enough. Now I was getting annoyed. I responded saying I wasn't interested right now, but I would be in touch when I was interested in learning more.

That didn't end things. For the next week, I received daily e-mails and voice mails. I unsubscribed from the e-mail list. Phone calls continued multiple times a week for the next 2 weeks. I blocked them. Finally, they stopped.

The company made the mistake of assuming because I downloaded the catalogue, I was ready to purchase. I was not. Although persistent, they were not patient, and they didn't listen to my requests. I was so turned off by the process, not only did I delete their catalogue, but I warned others who might fall into the same trap.

When someone expresses interest, especially online, that is only step one. Remember, it might take quite a few steps to get them to purchase. Walk with them at their pace, and you build trust. In the long term, that trust will bring you bigger sales and referrals than if you rushed them through the process.

# The 10 Commandments of Selling

*"I find it useful to remember, everyone lives by selling something"*

~ Robert Louis Stevenson

1. Do set big goals for yourself
2. Do stay healthy, positive, and optimistic
3. Do remain pleasantly, professionally persistent
4. Do learn to ask lots of good questions
5. Do vary your approach to each individual customer
6. Do confirm all conversations and agreements
7. Do take breaks to refresh yourself
8. Don't take anything for granted; anyone may be a customer
9. Don't assume anything in the sales process
10. Don't ever give up on yourself or your dreams

# Customer Service–Rule #1

*"Customers are no longer buying products and services—they are buying experiences delivered through the products and services"*

~ Gregory Yankelovich

We consumers buy so very many things that we actually don't want. We buy aspirin pills, concert tickets, and drill bits. But we do not really want a pill. While we may save the ticket stub as a souvenir, we don't really want a printed piece of paper. And we don't necessarily need a three-fourths-inch piece of hardware to throw in our toolbox. What we want is relief for our headache, admission to the stadium to hear the artist and the music, and a hole.

Our motivation to purchase items is not always about the object itself but rather what that object helps us accomplish, see, or do. *Why* is always more important than *what* in terms of human motivation. And purchasing habits.

Rule #1 of Customer Service is to understand why customers want what you have.

Customer satisfaction is the key benchmark for so many companies and industries. It cannot possibly be achieved without knowing what each individual customer needs your particular product and service to do for them. True customer service begins with a working knowledge about customer expectations regarding what value they are imagining by working with you.

We buy the car for dependable work transportation, family safety, or possibly prestige. We buy the dining-room table to entertain friends at, serve family meals at, and maybe double as an office desk. We buy the fancy sneakers to give us an advantage in an athletic competition, begin a long overdue fitness program, or perhaps just to look cool in school with.

Our marketing promise, promotions, and advertisements instantly create an expectation of service and value in the mind of a consumer. How well aligned our sales effort is with the marketing promise determines conversion and acquisition (sales). And the experience of the customer, based on the initial expectations created, ultimately determines customer satisfaction and loyalty.

Customer service begins with understanding why someone wants what you have. And then delivering the experience that the customer expects to receive because of buying from you.

One of my mentors used the example of a camera. "Why do you buy a camera?" he asked our group. We thought it might be a trick question so no one jumped to answer. Finally, a brave soul said in a very tentative voice, "To take a picture?"

"Really?" replied my mentor. "Is it really the picture you are looking to capture, or is it something more?"

Recently, I downsized my parents, and pictures were a heated topic of discussion. They wanted to keep all of them, but I really couldn't relate to the amateur pictures of their Alaska cruise. It just looked like a mountain, a bay, or a forest. I only wanted to keep the pictures of them and my grandparents. "You don't understand," said my father, "it was amazing to see the icebergs, mountains, and the villages."

I now realized sitting in this class, that he was right. I didn't understand. I wasn't there. The picture didn't mean anything because I didn't have an experience to attach to it.

"When we buy a camera," I stammered in class, "we are buying a way to capture an experience or memory. We aren't buying the camera or even the pictures it takes." My mentor smiled broadly and nodded.

On social, the same experience mind-set applies. People aren't coming to your website, or following you on Facebook, just to hear you pitch your stuff. They are coming for an experience. It could be some experience you offer them on your site or social channel, or it could be an experience they have when they visit.

Another way to look at it is they want the backstage pass. They want to see what goes on behind the scenes. They want to feel part of something beyond just your product or service.

This gets missed by most because they focus on the product or service only. If you look, however, at what is shared or what goes viral, you will find it reaches a different place, even if it is a brand talking.

By stepping back and asking yourself, *Why would someone want to buy my product or service? What experience are they truly seeking?* . . . You uncover the real reason they will come to you. Take that information and put it to use on social. Help them solve that problem by offering helpful advice. Give them the backstage tour through pictures on Instagram or Snapchat. Connect with them personally and get to know them.

Sometimes you don't even have to ask yourself the above questions. You can "listen" to what people are talking about regarding your industry, product category, or service. If you listen closely enough, you will hear the real reason they buy. Once you know that information, you have unlocked the secret door to engaging them.

# Customer Service Defined

*"Your customer doesn't care how much you know until they know how much you care"*

~ Damon Richards

Customer service begins with understanding why consumers want your product and service. It then moves to understanding their expectations around buying from you. And it achieves its goal when you continually exceed those expectations.

My definition of customer service is:

*The never-ending process of understanding and exceeding customer expectations in order to create both positive outcomes and loyal customer advocates.*

While all organizations must have repeatable business practices in order to replicate quality and job performance, there is a way to stand out in the customer service arena.

Don't provide even exceptional customer service. To make a real difference, provide *custom* service. Custom service always exceeds expectations.

We know that in the ultracompetitive business climate we all live in today, even meeting expectations may not be enough. It might only give us a 50/50 chance of retaining that customer. Certainly we know if we don't even meet expectations, the odds are significantly stacked against us. Only in exceeding the expectations of our clients do we give ourselves the best chance to have many satisfied, long-term relationships.

That alone should be enough of a motivation. But, even beyond that, customers who are delighted with their purchases become something more. They become loyal advocates of the organization and/or brand. And, those customers will be the most important marketing tool and de facto sales force you that can ever have. They will not be able to help but to tell all their friends about all the remarkable things that you do. And, if you can handle it, those loyal advocates whose expectations you exceeded will continue to generate a perpetual flood of new opportunities for you.

When you strive to *treat* customers a certain way rather than *handle* them a certain way, amazing things can happen. When they know you care by way of the "custom" customer service you provide, customers lower their guard and form real, meaningful bonds with you and your organization. And then, the competition becomes virtually irrelevant.

Thinking about consistently exceeding customers' expectations first means that you need to understand what they are.

In general, I think we can agree that we want the right product delivered at the right time for a fair price. We could also agree that we want to be treated with respect in a positive manner. In difficult situations, we might also expect to be communicated to in a timely manner, that the person who made the error fess up, and that some compassion is shown.

One tricky element is missing. I call that the "Unchecked Box." This is an expectation a customer has that is never stated, but can make—or break—the situation.

Take, for example, if you were going to eat at a fancy restaurant. Your customer experience checklist would include many of the qualities listed above, but what else might you expect that isn't on the list? Perhaps you desire to have the exact experience you had there 5 years ago, or maybe you hope they do something special for your father because you mentioned it was his 75th birthday.

The staff doesn't know you have these expectations. They aren't part of the standard checklist. We all, however, have these expectations tucked neatly away.

This is where social can help. By once again listening to what our customers and clients are talking about on social, we can better gauge our perceived level of service. We might also discover different ways to enhance the customer experience.

If you haven't heard the story of Peter Shankman and Morton's, it is a perfect example of what I am talking about.

Peter Shankman is speaker, author, and consultant, not to mention entrepreneur. He's highly engaged on social. You can follow him on Twitter at @PeterShankman. In August of 2011, Peter was flying back to Newark from Tampa. He casually tweeted *"Hey @ Mortons—can you meet me at newark airport with a porterhouse when I land in 2 hours? K, thanks. :)"* Morton's, by the way, is one of his favorite restaurants.

An amazing act of customer service happened at the Newark airport. Morton's showed up, not only with a porterhouse, but with a full meal! (You can read the full story here: http://shankman.com/the-best-customer-service-story-ever-told-starring-mortons-steakhouse/)

Morton's listens to their social channels. They pay attention because they know their customers are going to share some of those unspoken expectations there.

When building your social plan, you need to think about how you can leverage the conversations on social to learn more about your customers that will help you deliver that exceptional customer service.

# Protect Your Golden Geese

*"The best customer to have is the one you've already got"*

~ Dick Shaaf

Lead generation. Demand generation. Content marketing. Marketing automation. Social media. Advertising of all kinds . . . We spend enormous effort, energy, and money on finding new business. Organic growth of new customers through all manners of business development, strategies, and tactics. Obviously, almost no business can survive long term without continually adding new customers. But it does make me wonder. Do we spend the same kind of time, effort, and energy on protecting what we already have?

Unlike Aesop's telling of the story, I doubt that we are as greedy as the proverbial farmer with our existing customers and try to get everything we can out of them right away, only then to discard them. Instead, I think many of them simply go away out of neglect and perhaps an overly obsessive attitude on getting more customers instead of tending to the ones that we already have.

We've all been exposed to the statistics. Depending on which one you've seen, it costs anywhere from five to 12 times more to get a new customer than it does to keep the old one.

I read a white paper recently that stated the average company loses 10 percent of their customers each year. And that if they could reduce the attrition rate by as little as 5 percent, that overall profits could improve by anywhere from 25–95 percent, depending on the industry. Staggering. If anywhere near the truth, why do we sometimes allow for such ambivalence in our customer retention?

Our business relationships are no different than our personal ones. If the customer feels neglected, unattended, or worse yet, taken for granted, they will vote with their feet and find a new partner who treats them better . . . leaving you scrambling to fill the void and find a new customer to take their place.

All of your customers are unlikely to fall in what you would consider the ideal bucket. But, for the ones you want to keep, whether big or little fish, you must make them feel that they have an important place in your pond.

Good and smart customer retention is like a saying I heard once. "Make new friends but cherish the old; for one is silver, but the other one gold."

How many of your current customers are you following on your social channels? It is one of the most overlooked areas where you can add value and stay connected with your current customers and past customers.

Take, for example, a local florist. If they connected with each customer on Facebook, let's say, they would be able to see when their customers had significant life events, such as having a baby, that might warrant a surprise bouquet on their arrival home.

Or what if you are a business consultant and you followed your clients on Twitter. One day, they post about a new division. How great would it be if you followed up with your contact with a personal note congratulating them on their growth?

Social allows us to know in real time what is happening with our clients. "But we are so busy, how can we find the time to do all this?" you say.

My reply is you cannot afford *not* to do this for two reasons. First, your competition might be following your customers as well. If they send the flowers or the note, they may be perceived as more attentive. Suddenly, you find those loyal customers drifting in their direction.

Also, it provides for that ongoing relationship and future sales. As part of our strategy, we try to keep up with our customers as much as possible on social, whether it is sending a happy birthday message or commenting on something they post. The reward of continually showing up is additional sales. Customers may not purchase for a year or so, but again, when the need arises, we are the first people they call because they know we are there for them. They also know, if we have been doing our homework, that we already know what's happening in their business so there is less catch-up time required to solve their next problem.

Finally, a personal example. Recently, we changed from an online software company for our business to a competitor. The reasons? First, their customer support was nonexistent. Second, their program, although being regularly updated, started to feel outdated compared to their competition.

The final straw came from their website. To access the software, you had to sign in. The main page where you signed in was never without a special for new customers, such as 50 percent off your first year. When we inquired about possibly getting a discount, we were told no because we were an existing customer—an existing customer for nearly 6 years! They weren't able to reward a company who was loyal, but they were more than willing to reward a newcomer. We left the following month and have been extremely satisfied with our new provider!

Social combined with your online presence sends a strong message to your existing customers. It's important to do an audit of your activities and your promotions on a regular basis through the lens of your customers. Does what you promise encompass the long-term customer or is it just to lure new customers in? Do your actions online help to support your existing customers, or are they only directed toward new customers? These are important checkpoints that can help you redefine, if necessary, your social strategy.

# What Are You to Them?

*"Profit comes from repeat customers: those that boast about the product or service"*

~ W. Edwards Deming

The sign on the wall of my potential customer was shocking, and it got my immediate attention.

It described, in detail, how the organization graded potential suppliers. It read as follows:

| *Purely Competitive* | *Competitively based relationships* | *Differentiated Supplier* | *Strategic Alliance* |
|---|---|---|---|
| One-time buy | Mutually respectful | Close relationships | Very rare |
| Active competition | Many suppliers | Take time to develop | Very close |
| Quality is given | Active competition | Long term | |
| Short term | All have equal access | Limited vendors | |
| | | Risk sharing | |
| | | Quality focused | |

I was early in my sales career, but I got the message immediately. It really didn't matter what I thought that my products and services *should be* to them. The customer was going to get the final—and only—meaningful vote to decide where we fit on the matrix based on how they perceived our potential value.

I realized immediately that no one was going to be boasting about my value to them if they saw us only as a commodity or a one-time purchase that required active competition. It dawned on me that in my quest to find more customers, it was very important to find those that each party had the best chance to find ideal in terms of fit.

Your customer service will ultimately be almost meaningless if what you provide to your customer is not viewed by them as either vital to their business processes (i.e., a commodity) or different enough to truly stand out from the competition (requires active competition).

For your customer service to truly matter and help you retain customers over the long haul, you must have the courage and foresight to match up what you sell to someone who believes in what you do. They either believe in the power of relationships, if that's what you offer, or see your product and service as critical to their ultimate success, if that's truly what you have for them.

The value of what you offer will always be determined by the customer and the marketplace. The value that they perceive and/or how you make them feel always equals your report card.

Profit comes from repeat customers. Repeat customers are ideal customers. Customer service is best offered to and served on ideal customers, those that value your contribution and see you as an integral partner in their ultimate success.

## What Are You to Them?

The world of social, when you are engaged, gives you insight into what your customer values, and possibly how they view your products or services.

A good activity is to do a search of your company name through the social channels. Don't use your handle or your company page name. Instead, just search your company name. Notice what people are saying about you.

Now, do the same with your competitors, as well as your products or industry. You get a sense of when people felt there was a strong or weak relationship.

According to a report from Forrester Research, Inc., as described in the Ad Week article, Report: Facebook Likes Must Lead Fans To Purchase, Consider and Recommend Brands (http://www.adweek.com/socialtimes/likes-purchase-consider-recommend/391638), companies studied found a direct correlation between people who like a brand's Facebook company page and their purchasing activities. In summary, fans of a company's business page were, on average, 4–5.3 times more likely to purchase from that brand or company over nonfans.

When someone likes your business page, they are saying they want more of your information. Maybe they are in the research phase of the purchase. Maybe they have already purchased and want additional support. Maybe they have purchased in the past and want to know what's new.

No matter the reason they are saying they want the relationship to continue. These are the people who can help you understand the value they received from your product or service. Ask them, and then listen carefully. Try to remove your company biases and listen as if you are someone interested in your company. Notice what they talk about.

By leveraging these activities, you will have a better understanding of why your customer truly purchases your products or services. From there, you can continue to add value over the extended lifetime of the customer.

# How to Get an "A" at Customer Service

*"Courteous treatment will make a customer a walking advertisement"*

~ J. C. Penney

The statistics have been just about the same for the entire 30 years I've been in the business world. Based on almost every chart I've ever seen—here are the top reasons why your customers stop buying from you:

1. 1 percent pass away
2. 3 percent move
3. 14 percent are lured by a competitor
4. 14 percent are turned away by product or service dissatisfaction
5. 68 percent leave because of poor attitude or indifference on the part of the service provider

Put more simply—customers leave you when you *stop paying attention* to them.

Despite our ability and prevalence for choosing online shopping more than ever before, human beings are still very social creatures. That's why it is called *social* media. As social creatures, we still like praise, recognition, appreciation—in short—attention!

Ever walk into a store and be greeted by an associate? It doesn't have to be much. Just an acknowledgment that you are there and possibly a simple offer of help if needed. Ever walk into another store to see the employees standing around idly or talking among themselves, never looking up to even notice that you are there? If you've experienced both scenarios, then I bet I know which store you are more likely to buy from.

And probably keep buying from.

Being taken for granted is no way to begin, nurture, or sustain any relationship. We are hardwired with the need to get at least *some* attention, especially from those with whom we are spending our money. All things being equal, the organization that gives its customers more attention has a much-greater chance of creating and retaining customers than the one that gives limited or only sporadic attention. And what do customers who feel well taken care of do? They tell their friends about it . . . and you. And that creates more customers for your business.

As with all the important people in your life, if you want your customers to stay around, make sure you are giving them a high degree of quality attention on a regular basis.

Social has been labeled the new word-of-mouth marketing. Daily, people are asking for advice from friends, family, and to be honest, perfect strangers, who have become friends. Just connect to a local Facebook group, search a product on Twitter, or listen to your friends. You will hear questions asking for referrals from plumbers to books for summer reading.

The challenge of word-of-mouth marketing for businesses is you never know what people are saying or when they will be asking for your services. You can't take for granted that just because you did a great job for Customer A that he/she will remember you in a year when his/her friend asks for a referral.

Enter social. As we have been discussing, let's say you have been staying in touch with Customer A over the last 365 days. Let's also say you have been continuing to add value through social. When A's friend asks for a referral, you will naturally come to mind.

The problem, as we eluded to earlier, is, how you find the time to stay engaged?

The key is to have a plan. In addition to your social media marketing/sales plan, you need to have a social media customer service plan. This plan includes following and engaging with existing customers and clients. It also includes answering questions and, of course, handling any issues that come up.

A simple social media customer service plan is to set aside a certain amount of time per day to monitor your social channels. There are several online tools and paid services where you can bring all this data together.

If this seems like a lot of work, let me ask you this . . . If a customer called or e-mailed you with a question, would you ignore him? Of course not. You would do your best to answer the question, concern, or challenge.

The same thing is happening daily on social. People are asking questions about your product, or they are commenting about it. If you are there to chime in, you can stay engaged with those customers.

Try it yourself. First, ask your connections for a referral for a product or service. See what you get back. Next, make two comments about a product or service you recently purchased. One comment should tag the company or brand. The other comment just type their name into the comments.

Notice your results. How many of your friends or followers came back with some suggestions? Did the company you purchased from respond to either of your online comments?

You cannot control word-of-mouth marketing, but you can contribute to the conversation by valuing your customers for the long term and engaging on a regular basis.

# One Missing Sign Is Often the First of Many

*"Your most unhappy customers are your greatest source of learning"*

~ Bill Gates

I recently went to breakfast with a business colleague at a fairly large hotel restaurant. Now, if you're like me and most people that I know, when entering a restaurant, one tends to look for the sign that gives the instructions about how you're about to be served. It is both the first encounter and the first impression. The sign usually says either "please seat yourself" or "please wait to be seated." We looked behind the desk. We looked over toward the buffet line. We glanced over toward to seating area.

We saw no sign.

And to make things even more confusing, there was *no one* in any direction to help tell us what we should do. Not wanting to break the unwritten rule we did not see, we waited patiently with the expectation that someone would be right over. Staff was coming in and out of the kitchen with regularity. The front desk staff saw us standing there. So we waited.

And waited.

And waited some more.

After about 7 or 8 minutes, we made the executive decision to seat ourselves. The room was not particularly busy, and we were sure that someone would be right over to the table. After about another 7 to 8 minutes of patience and conversation, and now running tight on time to get to other meetings, we again made an executive decision and helped ourselves to the breakfast buffet. We put our coffee, juice, and first plate down at that table. Not seeing any silverware, we walked back to the buffet area to retrieve some. When we returned to our table, we found that our food had been cleared and that the table had been washed down!

While standing there more than somewhat both stunned and amused, a server suddenly and mysteriously appeared. When we mentioned what had happened, she very matter-of-factly responded that we could help ourselves to more food. And she disappeared again.

After finally reloading our plates and getting to sit with some food about 20 minutes or so after we had walked in initially, we found the eggs runny, the pancakes burned, the fruit not ripe, the coffee cold, and the juice warm. Adding all of these signs up, it explains completely why that particular place was just not busy. And probably wasn't going to be anytime soon.

Potential customers prejudge the likely service they will receive by many factors. They look for signs about your likely service experience to determine if you are worth spending their money on. Successful marketing is not only the ability to make prospects aware of your service, but more importantly, presents an appealing and attractive preview of coming attractions. Your marketing promise always creates customer service expectations in the mind of a customer.

Be obsessive about how well you greet—and treat—your customers. Understand that new potential customers are checking you out and watching very closely how you do things, even if you don't know they are. If you miss the mark with their first expectation, chances are that human nature will find other elements of your service that won't measure up. And they will most likely not come back again after a bad first experience. Or, not try you the first time if things don't look right to them while deciding. Just so you know, first impressions still count, *a lot*.

Customers have expectations about how they will be served. They look closely at how you do things and how other customers are being treated and what they say about their experiences with you. All the customer service signs you present add up eventually to a buy/no buy decision. What "signs" are *you* giving out?

Signs also extend to social. Have you ever been interested in potentially doing business with a company, or even met someone at a networking event and wanted to check them out online. You go to their website, it's ok, but doesn't wow you. You venture over to their Facebook business page, and you notice a series of similar posts, none of which are that interesting, and zero engagement and finally you head to Twitter, only to find much of the same. One strike was your website. Second strike your Facebook business page. Third strike your Twitter page . . . aaaannnnnd you're out! Oh, and by the way, that took less than 5 minutes to complete.

Recently, I wanted to give a colleague a recommendation of a caterer. I'd forgotten the actual business name, but knew I was connected to the chef on LinkedIn. I went to their LinkedIn profile to get their contact information, and the e-mail address wasn't valid. I checked out the website, and it led to a dead link. I finally tried the phone number, and it was out of service. Their LinkedIn presence told the story of a caterer out of business. Since I knew for a fact they were in business, and that it was thriving, I researched other ways to share their information.

My actions were unusual. Most would give up after the first or second failed attempt and move on. When I mentioned this to the caterer a few days later, he didn't seem too concerned. "It's only LinkedIn," he said. "It's not like my actual website was down."

That shortsighted thinking is easy to adopt, especially when you are a smaller business owner wearing multiple hats.

The moral to the story is you never know where your next customer is going to be looking for you. If they come across information that is not appealing, or flat-out wrong, they aren't going to be as persistent as was I. They are moving onto your competition because, like you, they don't have time to waste.

By paying attention to your online presence, by engaging with your audience through content relevant to their needs and lifestyles, by making it easy to learn more about you, you set the stage for future sales. Neglecting these tools or dismissing them as irrelevant because you "don't have time" is basically telling future customers you do not have time for them either.

On the flipside, another caterer I know embraces social. She considers the time she spends on Facebook as part of her marketing budget. She not only schedules time into her calendar to interact with her online community, but she realizes the financial cost of doing so and measures her investment with the return of her efforts.

She told me that her business has tripled by using Facebook. She's been able to meet, and engage with, people all over the United States, even though her business is local. Where some think that is a waste of time, she said, "You never know who people know. A woman I was helping in Columbus, Ohio, happened to have family here in Massachusetts. When her niece needed a caterer for a baby shower, the aunt in Columbus didn't hesitate to recommend the caterer. They got the job because of an out-of-state referral!"

What are *your* online signs telling others? Are you getting referrals from people out of state who have never physically met you, or are people passing you by because they imagine a "Gone Out of Business" sign on your virtual storefront?

# Are Your Customers a Problem—Or a Blessing?

*"There is only one boss. The customer. And he can fire everybody in the company from the chairman on down, simply by spending his money somewhere else"*

~ Sam Walton

Funny. I thought that at least if the customer wasn't always right, then at the very least, they would not be thought of as an annoyance to the customer service person taking their money!

I got the call on my way back from work. The message was that one of my kids needed a present for a birthday party they were going to that night. So much for advanced planning. Not wanting to guess at what this particular little girl might want, I opted for the least common denominator and decided to go for the all-purpose "gift card." After all, that ensured that she could pick out just what she wanted without any disappointments.

Needing to pick up a few food items on the way anyway, I decided to go into the nearest Big Box store to complete the birthday present transaction and food grab in one stop. A quick trip up and down a few aisles produced some fruit, milk, cookies, and cereal tucked neatly into my basket. I quickly picked out a universal gift card from the display and headed to the nearest checkout counter.

The checkout clerk looked particularly rumpled. Enthusiasm to be attending the register was not my first impression. My attempts at pleasantries were not returned. Chalking it up to that this person was having a bad day, I thought nothing more about it as the food items got rung up without issue. I was determined to maintain my good attitude, check out quickly, and whisk the birthday present home with alacrity to make sure it could make its way to the party on time.

After I had bagged the food items, it came time for the gift card activation. After the first swipe, I kindly pointed out to the cashier that she had charged me *double* than my intended amount. "Humph" came the response.

The second attempt brought with it a long sigh when I mentioned that this time she had keyed in the wrong amount. The third attempt did not provide the desired result either when she then could not get the card to activate at all. "You know," she said to me in a disgusted tone, "I'm getting really annoyed!"

She finally was able to get the deal done the way I had asked for initially, to which my response was, "I'm sorry to have annoyed you." To which her response was another louder and deeper "Humph." I picked up my bags, tucked the gift card in my jacket pocket, and wished her a good night. A blank stare and no response was all I got in return.

Do you think her boss, manager, or the store's owner would like me to mention the name of that store? I'm guessing not. Do they know the negative impact of an unpleasant transaction? And the number of people that will be told about the dissatisfaction with a transaction, store, or an associate?

J. Willard Marriott got it right a long time ago when he regularly preached to his managers to "Take care of your associates and they'll take care of your customers." I wonder how well-trained and well cared for the employees of that particular store are. Although based on that one experience, I already have a guess.

Stating the obvious, just so you know, don't take your customers for granted—they are your boss. "Thank you for shopping with us," "I appreciate your patience," and, "Please come again" still work wonders to make customers feel good and appreciated. And even an "I'm sorry that didn't go smoothly" when necessary goes a long way to smooth ruffled feathers.

I won't be a problem for that store again.

Because I won't be going back.

You can create a similar experience for your customers when they want to engage with you online, but you take no notice.

A well-known local restaurant did just that. After a disappointing anniversary dinner, a friend of mine posted a comment on their Facebook page. It wasn't a terrible comment. She just said she was disappointed in their experience, especially because they were celebrating a special event.

Then there were crickets. Nothing. Nada. The Inn never responded to her post.

Although professing to deliver exceptional customer service, they dropped the ball in this situation. Literally 6 months later another person went to their page to ask a question about their experience. They saw my friend's unanswered post. Again, the post wasn't crazy, angry, or outrageous. What was outrageous was that in 6 months the restaurant never responded!

Instead of posting their comment, the new person asked why they didn't respond to my friend's post because they had a similar experience. Perhaps because we were heading into the busy summer season, the restaurant was more attentive to the second person. They apologized to them for their negligence. That was a good first step.

Next, they contacted my friend to find out what happened. She was shocked. It had been so long, her memory of it was a little cloudy. She recalled the story to the best of her ability. The response was that they had a complete turnover in staff and they would welcome her and her husband back for dinner.

That's all good, right? Sounds like they just slipped up and were trying to make it right, but here's the clincher. At the end of the conversation, they made sure to mention, "Oh, by the way, can you go back to Facebook and post something positive?"

Now, this can be a good tactic . . . when it is done in a timely manner. How do you think my friend felt? Even if the restaurant was sincere in their outreach efforts, the last comment negated all that good work.

Stuff happens in our businesses. Product ships late. You are down a waitstaff. You just got your biggest order ever, and it's pushing all the other work around. If you are honest with your customers, they will understand. If you have done your customer service recovery well and in a timely manner, they will want to share that experience.

As much as business fears the negative comments of their customers online, and there are some who take it to the extreme, the fact is, if your customer has a bad experience, they are already telling their friends and family, or writing about it in a book. Wouldn't you rather they say something to you on social? At least you can respond and make it right.

In the past, we weren't always aware what our customers were saying about our products and services. With social, we can repair the broken relationship and potentially create a customer for life.

# Fishing for a Customer Service Pro

*"Whatever you do, do it well. Do it so well that when people see you do it they will want to come back and see you do it again, with their friends"*

~ Walt Disney

In my mind, selling and customer service are very close to the same thing in a retail setting. B2B salespeople have to go out and find customers. They need to do much more outbound activity. Retail salespeople have the advantage of having the prospective customer come to them.

I was never much of a fisherman, though I used to catch a few carp, bass, and pickerel as a teenager on the small pond that I grew up near.

But I know good presentation and good salesmanship/customer service when I see it. And that's exactly what I found on my first encounter in a Bass Pro Shop store on a recent random visit. Visiting with a colleague who was looking for some poles for his family's upcoming vacation, I was quickly overcome with the savvy marketing and sales professionalism of this successful chain.

It became readily apparent that although my friend knew very little about fishing, he was being handled by a pro, working for a very sophisticated marketing and sales organization. I immediately noticed three very specific traits that are common to all successful businesses.

*Creating favorable selling conditions.* The moment you walk in the front door, you are feeling the excitement. The Bass Pro Shop is a virtual cornucopia of sights and sounds, a very real stimulus to your senses. From the well-conceived displays to the video hunting games to the giant fish tank, running stream, and stuffed wild animals, it had it all. Their overall appearance was very professional, but it had the feeling "fun" stamped all over it.

In our hectic, stressed, and look-alike world, Bass Pro Shops is able to create an environment where you can actually enjoy spending your time (and money) being engaged and informed. As our personal attention spans decrease, so too does a marketer's or salesperson's ability to get noticed. In marketing and sales, boring is death. If you can't attract and hold attention, you won't make many sales. And you'll keep fewer customers.

Think about how you market your business and ask yourself these questions:

- How well do you create favorable selling conditions for every customer interaction?
- Does your store, Web site, or literature convey professionalism yet also a feeling of "fun"?
- How much excitement, education, or involvement do you have in your selling process?

To attract fish—you need appealing bait.

*Advising the customer on what they truly need rather than what they think they need.* The mark of a true pro is not to "take the order" the way the customer thinks he or she may want it, but rather, having the knowledge and confidence to ask questions and uncover what's truly best for each customer's individual situation.

My friend was ready to walk out with the "off-the-shelf" reasonably priced version of a basic pole. The sales associate was clever enough to ask some questions that quickly showed that was not the right tool to do the job. The poles were for my friend's two sons, age 9 and 10. The salesperson asked how old the boys were, how tall they were, where they would be fishing, what they would be fishing for, and if they were fishing to "keep 'em" or throw them back. After spending just a few minutes inquiring about the conditions and the results that my friend was hoping for, he was able to suggest other equipment that, while slightly more expensive, was the proper "fit" to do the job. And the sale went from $60 to *$160*—in the blink of an eye!

Judge your sales performance with these three questions:

- How often do you simply "take the order" without asking the customer any questions?
- Do you spend more time selling—or—more time informing, educating, and asking what the specific needs of your customers are?
- When you do realize that what they want is not what they need, do you have the courage to tell them?

To catch the fish—you have to know how to set the hook.

*Making them happy they spent the money.* The mark of a truly successful organization is having each customer walk away happy with his or her purchase and being glad they parted with their money to obtain it. And come back another time for more. How many of us come out of store and feel the pangs of buyer's remorse almost immediately? Or, after owning something for some time, we don't feel that we got "our money's worth"? Or, after something does not work or function as expected, we receive less than satisfactory customer service if we raise an issue?

From my brief encounter there, it became obvious in overhearing the conversations of other customers that they had been to a Bass Pro Shop and purchased other products before. And they were back for more. One look at their Web site, special offers, reward programs, and ease of use made me a believer in the serious mission they have to build and retain a loyal customer base, what Ken Blanchard talked about in one of my favorite books, *Raving Fans.*

If you are experiencing retention issues, ask yourself these questions:

- Do you know who your repeat customers are and why they continue to buy from you?
- When was the last time you surveyed them for their opinions and feedback about you?
- Do you make it easy and tangibly encourage and thank them for continuing to buy from you?

Fish may not jump in the boat—but—there are ways to reel them in time after time.

My friend told me after his vacation he actually went back to the store and sought out the salesperson to tell them how much he appreciated his advice. The boys had a great time and caught lots of fish.

Enticing, catching, and landing fish takes time, patience, skill, and commitment. So does attracting, acquiring, and retaining customers.

With that experience in mind, look at your online and social presence. If you are near your computer, do it now. I'll wait.

Are you creating a favorable, in the eyes of your customer, buying experience? By this, I mean, can they find the answers to their questions? Is it easy to purchase or is your shopping cart outdated, and it takes them several clicks to complete a purchase?

Thinking about the environment, does your online and social presence appeal to your ideal customer? Is it engaging, stimulating, and even entertaining? Do they see other people who have purchased in the past sharing their enthusiasm? Not sure what this looks like? Check out the Zappos Facebook page. You can't help but being drawn in by the enthusiastic responses from the fans of the page. One woman called the customer service reps at Zappos her friends, and then went on to name them. It feels like a cool place to hang out. How does your online presence stack up?

Next, are you advising your customers through your online and social presence? I don't mean advising them of your upcoming sale, but helping them, answering questions, suggesting solutions?

Engagement is the new word-of-mouth marketing. When you engage authentically with your customers online, they want to share their experience, or at least what they learned. If you are only fostering one-way communication, you to them, you are missing out on some great customer service opportunities to connect in a more meaningful way with current and potential customers.

Every day, people are posting questions you may be able to answer. The question is, are you online and paying attention enough to be there?

By offering advice and answering questions, you open the door for further conversations. Gary Vaynerchuk did this religiously and built his wine business. He continues to do it, now even inviting questions about business and marketing in this new world.

Finally, does your online presence or social activity help customers feel happy they spent their money? This is where e-mail marketing becomes a crucial part of your customer service social strategy. When used correctly, a well-timed and authentic e-mail after purchase can make the customer slide right through buyer's remorse and into delighted customer.

I'm not talking about the canned responses we normally get with a link to a survey about your experience. This e-mail speaks directly to the person, calling them by name, referencing what they purchased, and even what to expect when they receive delivery.

E-mail marketing, when done correctly, cements the relationship you want to have with your customer. It makes them feel special. It makes them feel as though because they purchased from you, they are in the inner circle.

Use this tool carefully, however. It might be tempting to continue to communicate what you want to sell to them in the future, but that is where most e-mail marketing/customer relationship marketing goes astray. You want to keep in touch with them, but on their terms. Connecting on subjects important to them, providing them with a channel to communicate, and involving them gives them an experience they will remember and share with others.

# Santa's Customer Service Secrets

*"This is the ultimate in feel-good projects. To make money and make people happy; it's a Santa Claus project"*

~ Craig Belser

Santa Claus may just preside over the most successful customer service organization in the world. This is amazing, given the fact that he has many logistical and operational disadvantages.

The ordering system is antiquated. It does not rely on either speed or ease of order entry. It is driven by and handles good old-fashioned snail mail. Nothing automated or bar-coded to enter once the request has arrived. Each letter must be read individually. Production processing is not equipped with modern machine advantages, based on what I'm told. It still depends on a skilled manual-labor workforce to build all the toys. And delivery does not benefit from a fleet of planes, trains, or automobiles. Or any sophisticated GPS tracking capability. Santa is still able to do it all in just one sled, on one night, pulled by reindeer.

And yet, despite having very few, if any, competitive advantages, from initial request to order fulfillment, Santa brings joy to millions of perfectly satisfied customers every year.

Here's three things that I've noticed he does that all of us could do well to emulate.

1. Santa Built an Enthusiastic Team. I've been told that the elves are the most happy and satisfied workers in the world. They are treated well. The have a concrete and well-defined mission. They work with a purpose and sense of urgency. They work hard at their craft to become world-class at what they do. The elves share happily in the satisfaction and delight of their customers. Customer experience is almost always enhanced when an organization makes these levels of commitment. Happy (talented, appreciated, and committed) workers make happy customers.
2. Santa Has Perfect Order Accuracy. Have you ever heard of someone getting the wrong item in the package that they had ordered from Santa? I haven't. All that needs to happen is for the customer to send one letter to the post office at the North Pole and your request is immediately entered into the system, no follow-up required. Customers don't need to exert any extra effort to get what they ordered initially. On the rare occasions that someone has changed their mind, he's arranged with JC Penney, Walmart, and other fine retailers to take back returns and make exchanges. That's more convenient than bringing things back to his workshop.
3. Santa Has Perfect On-time Delivery. I've never heard of anyone getting anything late from Santa. His sled does not pull up with the UPS or USPS trucks on December 26th, or, later. No back order or out-of-stock notifications. Nothing that needs to take excessive time, effort, or consternation to track and follow where and when packages might arrive. He always makes sure

to hit the promised delivery date of December 25th. That ensures that he or his staff will never have to deal with listening to customer complaints about missing critical deliveries.

If we can build a happy workforce, dedicated to customer satisfaction, and deliver the right item to the right customer at the right time, we can be thought of as having a world-class operation—just like Santa Claus.

All of this happens because Santa Claus has a customer-centric organization. To be customer-centric, everything revolves around the customer. All operational, hiring, and product decisions are made with the customer in mind. It is not enough to come up with a great idea they think kids would love; they learn what kids love, and then deliver that. This is how Santa gets the buzz he does all year long.

By focusing his organization on the customer and holding them to high standards, Santa can boast that, according to a study done by Unversity of Texas psychologist, Jacqueline Woolley http://www.theatlantic.com/health/archive/2014/12/when-do-kids-stop-believing-in-santa/383958/, over 82 percent of 5-year-olds believe in him. That is much better than the American Express Global Customer Service Barometer http://about.americanexpress.com/news/pr/2014/outstanding-service-spend-more-spread-word.aspx, which said in 2013 that only 5 percent of companies exceeded the test group's expectations.

Another factor Santa has going for his customer-centric organization is the ability to speak with him, or possibly a helper, face-to-face, in nearly every mall across America, not to mention hospitals, local service organizations, and even at a Christmas party. The Global Customer Service Barometer confirmed this:

> *Even in a digitally connected world, consumers' preferred method for talking about their service experiences is still face-to-face conversation. Nine in ten consumers say they tell others face-to-face about their service experiences—good or bad.*

What does this mean for your digital efforts?

First, develop a Customer-centric Commitment Statement. Articulate your promise to your customers online and off-line in a simple statement your entire organization can get behind. At the North Pole, they may have a statement like "We promise to make all children happy."

Use your Customer-centric Commitment Statement as the foundation for your social and traditional marketing plan, as well as in your decision-making processes. Continue to refer to it as you define goals, choose channels, and develop content.

This Customer-centric Commitment Statement drives your interactions as well. With social being the new word-of-mouth marketing, people will share their experiences. Let's say a person has a good experience and tells one person. That same person, when they have a negative experience, will tell three people. That's a lot of bad press neither Santa's Village nor your company can endure over the long term. With many of those people now taking those comments to social, they live for the long term and can affect others' purchasing decisions.

When your Customer-centric Commitment Statement drives your interactions, you are empowered to respond to the customer in a way that meets their needs. As this process is repeated, you develop a reputation that can last for centuries.

> *"Service, in short, is not what you do, but who you are."* ~ Betsy Sanders, author, *Fabled Service: Ordinary Acts, Extraordinary Outcomes*

By adopting and embracing a customer-centric organizational style, Santa has grown his humble operations to a worldwide enterprise over the last 500–600 years. That's a pretty good track record, don't you think?

# How to Lose a Lifelong Customer in Under 10 Seconds

*"One customer well taken care of could be worth more than $10,000 worth of advertising"*

~ Jim Rohn

I tallied it up before I walked in. I had purchased almost every item of furniture that I owned from this particular store for nearly 25 years. Bedroom and dining-room sets. TV armoires. End tables. Coffee tables. At least a half-dozen couches. I guessed somewhere well north of $30,000 over those 25 years. Eight kids and two houses' worth of stuff.

So when I walked in with two pillows recently that had "not quite worked out for me," I was sure that I would be treated as both the valued long-term customer and advocate of the business that I was. After all, they had been great to me every time I had made a purchase.

Was I the biggest customer in their portfolio? Of course not. But I thought that based on all the loyalty that I had shown them, and the business I had given them over the years, that I'd have the chance to get some satisfaction to which had been a very unsatisfactory purchase.

Here is what I got instead. I walked in with the two pillows (one still sealed in the original packaging, the other not because I had taken it out) to the front desk. The "greeter" said that he could not help me but instructed me that I could go back to bedding section where someone would "be happy" to assist me. So I walked through the entire length of the 250,000+ square foot building to find five associates sitting on a couch talking with one another. One eager young gentleman jumped up and asked if he could help. "Yes," I said, "I got these pillows from you awhile back and—" "I'm sorry, sir," came his immediate response, "we can't take back pillows, *it's company policy.*"

I assured him that I understood and mentioned my lifetime of purchases, but before I could finish my sentence (again), up jumped the on-duty store manager and said very authoritatively to her team, "I'll handle this."

"Sir, there is nothing we can do. It's a hygiene situation. We simply cannot take back any pillows." I was not quite 10 words into my response saying how I understood that they could not take back opened pillows when I was, once again, interrupted midsentence. "As I've already explained, there is nothing we can do for you," she said—emphatically! And in the process, raised her hand showing me toward the door.

Well, by my reckoning, how it felt was that I had now been both poked in the eye with a sharp stick and kicked in the shin with a heavy boot. By a company that I had given lots and lots of my hard-earned money to.

Was this a fly-by-night-operation? Far from it. Largest furniture store in the area. Commercials on every TV channel. Faces on billboards on every highway. Great reputation and up until now in my experience, great customer service.

Here's the ironic thing. I had no expectation of being able to return the pillows. It had been more than 2 months since I had purchased them. I had taken one out of its packaging to test with a pillow case and towel over it when I got home (something I did not try to hide). I *totally* get the hygiene thing. I wouldn't want to be wearing someone else's used bathing suit, underwear, or anything else that someone used and returned, for that matter. I simply wanted to know what the store could, *and would*, do for *me*. For someone who had been both a very loyal customer and strong advocate for a very long time.

I walked to the door and out into the cold dark parking lot with my tail between my legs, feeling more than a little beat up.

Somewhat flabbergasted, but now coming to my senses, I even called back later after a number of minutes to ask one last time if they would consider doing anything for me. "Mr. Butler, I do not appreciate being bullied" came the response from the on-duty manager.

Was I a great customer that night? Probably not. It was the end of a very long day. I was more than a little tired and cranky. Not that I ever hope to use that as an excuse for poor behavior. I fully admit that I was probably more than normally a bit testy and challenging.

But after much soul searching, I'm confident to say that I do not believe that I "started it." As a customer, all I wanted was a little understanding and an offer of help. Not the iconic NO that I got stuck in my face.

On multiple occasions.

Did the manager do her job? In the most basic of ways, I suppose yes. Did she follow her training? Tough question. I'm guessing that she did. Would senior management and ownership be happy with how the situation was handled? I'm really not sure. Probably yes. Was I an annoying customer on that particular night? I probably was. Did they lose me as a customer? And any and all future referrals? 100 percent yes!

Why? Because there were so very many ways not to. How about some questions? Do you understand why we can't take these back (get me involved)? What would you like us to do (ask my opinion)? Is there anything we could do to make you happy (give me the chance for some relief and satisfaction)?

I would have been beyond satisfied with a $25 gift certificate or something similar. I don't believe that would be a lot to offer for a $150 purchase that I was disappointed with and would never use. Something, *anything* to show that you spent some effort on me and not only left the door open for me to come back, but to find a way to turn a problem into a sales opportunity.

But I never even got the chance. Everyone was just way too eager to pull out and hide behind the "company policy" card as a way to shoot me down. Before I had even asked for anything.

I just didn't want to be told what I was told. That there was *nothing* that could be done for me. That there was no way to satisfy the *buyer* because the *seller* had to come first. Not for someone who had been a loyal customer for over 25 years.

The second ironic thing. I had purchased two other pillows, still sealed in their original packaging, that were sitting in my trunk that night. Despite my earlier dismissal, I summoned the courage to walk into Bed, Bath & Beyond. I prepared myself for what I assumed would be a similar rejection to another seemingly and experientially ludicrous request on my part. "Hi, I bought these pillows from you a while back and—"

"No problem, sir" came the response. "Do you have the card which you purchased them with?" And in 2 minutes, I walked out with a complete purchase refund on those two pillows.

Care to guess where I will be shopping from now on? And where I won't be?

*"While 46% of American consumers say they always tell others about good service experiences, an even greater number say they talk about poor service experiences. In fact, 60% said they always share the bad ones, and they tell nearly three times as many people (an average of 21 people vs. 8 people)."* ~ American Express Global Customer Service Barometer, http://about.americanexpress.com/news/pr/2014/outstanding-service-spend-more-spread-word.aspx

Why are we more inclined to tell people or write about our negative versus our positive experiences?

It's simple. We are trying to save people the wasted expense, be it time or money, on a product or service that was subpar. We are trying to be helpful.

From a business perspective, these situations, on the surface, seem anything but helpful, especially when it comes to social media. In fact, it can hold a company back from exploring social as a marketing channel because they don't want to "open a can of worms" providing a space for customers to complain in public.

Let's think about this for a second.

If a customer has an experience that doesn't meet their expectation, they are going to tell people about it no matter what. It could be in a casual conversation, or even worse, just as a person is prepared to buy. They are going to share their experience whether you have a Facebook page or not.

Let's say in this situation they happened to tell a friend and you overheard. What would you do?

Some of you might engage in the conversation to find out more and possibly offer some solutions. Others might not feel comfortable jumping into another conversation, but I would venture to guess all of you would make a mental note to check into it when you were back at the office. You might not be able to help the person directly. You may, however, be able to look at the system or process to avoid it happening in the future.

Social provides this opportunity. Now you don't have to lurk around listening to conversations at the next barbeque. Your customers might tag you in a conversation or reach out to you directly with their situation. You then have the chance to find out more before they go off to tell others online and off-line. You can address the issue more directly with the customer *and* with your organization.

The key principle is remembering people want to be heard. It's a best practice not to have the conversation on social, but direct it to the person off-line to better understand their situation.

In many cases, people will take to social with their comments because it is easier than calling a 1-800 number and listening to endless Muzak. In many cases, they don't expect a response. I know I didn't when I recently posted to an airline about how they handled a flight. And usually their expectations are met, and the company never responds.

Think about the customer service power you can have when you do respond. Not only are you able to humanize your company, but you can find out what truly is working in the eyes of the customer and what is not.

Ultimately, if the customer has one too many of these negative experiences, they will disappear. You are then left to try to understand why sales are down. Wouldn't it be better to interact with your end user early on? The internal fix might be smaller than you think. One post on Facebook may save your company hundreds, if not thousands or tens of thousands, of dollars in the end.

# Leave the Pillow Fights for Sleepovers

*"Although your customers won't love you if you give bad service, your competitors will"*

~ Kate Zabriskie

A funny thing happened on the way to customer (*dis*)satisfaction.

I truly do not think of myself as a terribly difficult person. I think that people who really know me well would say that while extremely competitive, that I'm not a whiner or complainer (I hope). And over my 50+ years I can probably count on one hand how many times I have gotten really upset over customer service to the point of exasperation.

This "pillow talk" situation was truly my pinnacle of customer dissatisfaction.

As I mentioned in the previous chapter, I had a very dissatisfactory experience with my long term store of choice for furniture store. I added it up more accurately just after the previous events just for fun. I had spent over $40,000 in purchases with them over the last 25 years. And what no one that evening was aware of was that I was in the process of moving and in the market for a bedroom set, couch, and other odds and ends. On the verge of more than $5,000 of new furniture purchases.

Not that she knew, but none of that mattered to, or maybe not even occurred to, the manager anyway, who insisted that they could not help me in any way over a $75 pillow.

I was angered, frustrated, and disappointed. Emotions that I don't have often and try steadfastly to avoid. That's when I had a flash of inspiration. A few days later, I took the offending pillows back to another store in the chain, receipt again in hand. I walked in without expectation and was greeted warmly by two associates, the second of whom walked me right over to the customer service desk. Up jumped the customer service manager to ask how she could help. I explained that I had tried the first pillow for a couple of nights but that it had actually hurt my neck. And relayed that I had no need for the other pillow (again, still hermetically sealed) and was wondering—But before I could finish my story, the customer service manager said . . . "No problem, sir, we'd be happy to give you a refund." In under 3 minutes, I walked out without the felonious pillow in my possession and with $79.88 refunded to my credit card.

Say what?!

How could one store in the same chain say no and one store say yes? How could one manager in the same chain handle the situation so well and the other handle it so poorly? Now I was truly perplexed.

Feeling guilty about how I may have handled the situation at the first store, I stopped at the other location on my way back home and went to the customer service desk and asked if I could speak to the manager. I was pleased when they paged the same person I had encountered previously to the come see me. I even remained optimistic after the third page and waiting more than 10 minutes for her to come by.

My enthusiasm vanished when she walked up to me with a disgusted look on her face, which she did not try to hide, apparently recognizing me as she strode up. I introduced myself and reminded her of the "situation" we had the other night. I apologized if I was out of line and had given her a hard time. "Uh-huh" was her only response. Then I hit her with my question. "I just took the pillow back to another one of your stores and they gave me a full refund. And I'm just wondering why they could give me a refund and why you wouldn't?" To which came the worst response to a customer I think that I've ever heard. *"I'm sorry, sir, but it's really none of your business how we do things!"*

Say what?!

What customer buying any product or service doesn't take into consideration both how and why a supplier does things? It is an enormous part of the buying process. And quite probably, the greatest determination of long-term customer loyalty and retention.

I had gone from disappointed and frustrated to satisfied and feeling cared for—to utterly dismissed (again) in about 1 hour.

I'm still left with more questions than answers. Why was this particular manager so hostile, twice? Who handled the situation properly in the eyes of ownership, store one or store two? Was I wrong with how I handled it, twice?

Bottom line #1. The store again lost a customer that they had just been able to win back.

Bottom line #2. Good customer service almost always gets rewarded. And poor customer service loses customers—always. And to me at least, it seems very silly to give up any amount of money and goodwill over something so very minor that could have been handled so very differently.

She may not have meant it in terms of customer service but the words of Maya Angelou are deadly accurate in terms of business development and relationship management. "I've learned that people will forget what you said, people will forget what you did, but people will never forget how you made them feel."

Whether we are a microbusiness consisting of ourselves or a larger organization, consistency in customer service expectations is paramount. *Presocial media*, that meant customer service training for sales staff and the customer service department for the proactive company.

Today, as we have been discussing, every employee is in the customer service department because they have access to social media. They have the power to engage with our current and future customers. Unfortunately, the care we might have taken when it was only one or two departments to ensure our customer service standards were understood . . . does not always happen.

Social media empowers the customer to learn about and communicate with your company on all levels. If *all* employees don't understand the customer service expectations and how to handle themselves online as a representative of the company, you may have problems well beyond the "pillow talk" situation.

Certainly, management must understand and consistently communicate the same customer service expectations, but now, you need to think about the others in your company. What about the warehouse worker, administrative assistant, even a temporary or virtual employee? Each of these people have the opportunity to connect with your customers on social media. They may not even be aware they are doing so!

I am certainly not saying you need to dictate how employees act on social media outside of the company, but you *do* need to think about communicating the importance of their position, no matter what it is. You need to motivate them to represent the company and themselves in the most positive light. And, if they choose to use social media as a communication vehicle with friends and family, how to do so properly.

Ultimately, if you find you have a customer service issue online, it is about addressing that with the company and the individual.

*"In the world of Internet Customer Service, it's important to remember your competitor is only one mouse click away."* ~ Doug Warner

# An 800 Number is NOT Customer Service

*"You'll never have a product or price advantage again. They can be too easily duplicated. But a strong customer service culture can't be copied"*

~ Jerry Fritz

The computerized voice on the other end of the line sounded so convincing. "We so value your business. Thank you for your call, it is very important to us." Then, suddenly, while I was punching in my account number, the call was disconnected.

I call back. The same lovely greeting. The same entering of account information. The same being hung up on again. And just for good measure, a third time as well.

The fourth time was a bit of a charm. I managed to navigate the account number input. I was offered a host of options. Push #1 for this. Push #2 for that. Unfortunately, none of the options were what I was looking for. So I pushed "0." Invalid entry I was told.

I tried a few more times but once again was disconnected.

Fifth try. I decided to simply push #1 in hopes of getting to a real live person. Three more suboptions awaited me. Finally, I got someone on the line who sounded about as happy as someone whose car may have blown up on the way to work. Next came the clincher for me. "What is your account number, sir?" "Why have I entered it five times and you cannot identify who I am?" I asked. This time, I hung up. And found someone new to do business with.

Retaining customers is not a birthright. It is not inevitable. It is not an entitlement. The right to continue the business relationship is something that must be perpetually earned. With every encounter. With every transaction. How you leave your customer feeling after you've interacted with them is, and always will be, your ultimate report card.

Providing the "basics" and being comparable to anyone in your industry is not enough. Never be satisfied with "good enough." If your customer does not feel a little bit better after interacting with you than they felt just before, beware.

I once worked with someone who had something interesting to say after a meeting with a customer that was a bit tense. They were asking us to stretch a bit and provide something just beyond our normal service. The comment was, "Well, what the customer has to understand is . . ." Hmm. I'm all for negotiation. I'm not sure about customer capitulation. What the customer knows is that there are many companies who can service them. And many who will stretch, give more, and go the extra mile to earn the business. And to keep it.

And all of them have an 800 number, I'm sure. The organization who wins the business both now, and in the future, is going to have to continually provide much more than just the basics.

The 800-number thought process also carries to social media. As we have been talking about, people will take to social with a question or potentially a complaint many times before they call that insidious 1-800 number. Why? The hope is that the company will reply to them there.

But alas, the company only set up their account to push content out to others. They don't want people to reach out there, so like the preverbal ostrich, they bury their head in the sand, not monitoring their brand across social channels. A perfect example are companies who have a Twitter account, but in the name of efficiency, they connected their Facebook to Twitter. Whatever they post on Facebook magically appears on Twitter. They think they are "doing" social.

Now, let's say a customer wants to let you know about a situation. Maybe they have even tried to call your 800 number, but did not get very far. They are on Twitter and notice you have an account, so they decide to tweet to you about their situation.

Since you aren't active on Twitter, you have no idea they want to talk with you. It's the same as getting lost in the automated voice system or having the phone disconnected. How do you think the customer feels now? Even if their issue was small to start, the fact they can't get a hold of you grows their dissatisfaction.

Here's the deal . . . Your customers are going to talk, and they are going to talk on whatever channel they feel comfortable. If you choose to have an account on a social channel, it is your obligation, if you value your customers, to pay attention to the channel.

Social channels are first and foremost social. They are designed to create conversation. Conversation requires two people to happen. When you choose to use it as a one-way communication vehicle, you are missing the fundamental premise on which the platform was designed.

Companies who embrace the notion of conversation on social channels can provide their present and future customers with a special experience that can make them advocates. Companies who choose to use their social networks as broadcast channels create opportunities every day for their customers to disengage, leave, and connect with their competition.

# The Five Fundamentals of Great Customer Service Organizations

*"Quality in a service or product is not what you put into it. It is what the customer gets out of it"*

~ Peter Drucker

Like any discipline in life, there are some basics, some building blocks, some fundamentals of service that must be in place in order to create and sustain a superior position in the mind and hearts of your customers.

1. They act out of faith and not fear. They believe in the relationship that they have with their customers and do not worry about being taken advantage of. This allows those organizations to have fewer cumbersome rules and less burdensome red tape. In addition, they empower their employees to make decisions in the best interest of the customer which engenders speed and loyalty.
2. They act with consistency and decisiveness. They know both what they stand for and what they deliver. Staying on point allows them to deliver purposeful service and to develop a brand

that is comfortable, familiar, and sharable.

3. They act with a sense of authenticity. If necessary, they "lost the suit." Relationships are built between like-minded people. Style, personality, and creativity are all encouraged. Support of common values allow the organization's unique spirit to come out and be shared with the customer.
4. They provide "custom" service. They understand that a one-size-fits-all service effort actually only fits a few, not the many. They take the time to get as intimate as possible with each customer's specific needs, wants, and desires. And to the best of their ability, they customize each customer's experience.
5. They act with radical sincerity. If a mistake is made, they apologize quickly. They do not leave the customer hanging, waiting for a resolution. It is understood that despite any automated technology that might have been used to place an order, that the relationship with the customer still ultimately exists between people. Maintaining (or restoring) a relationship with their customers is always the highest priority.

While there may be many layers of strategy and tactics woven into the execution of the customer service plan, these five elements will always be at the core of the best customer service companies.

If you want your organization to become customer-centric, these five elements are the cornerstones of engaging your employees and your customers. Let's look at how these translate to the world of customer service on your social channels.

> Act out of faith not fear—Companies who embrace their customers online, respond, and engage with them are acting out of faith rather than fear. They create trust through conversation. They also

embrace newer technology. Instead of fearing the never-ending changes and updates to the platforms, they look at the new advantages they have to reach their customers.

Act with consistency and decisiveness—Customer-centric companies show up on a regular basis for their customers on their social channels. Their customers look forward to their posts because they feel the company is speaking directly to them. Because of their relationship, the customers also feel when they do reach out in a one-on-one conversation with a question or issue, the company, their friend/partner, will be there to help. They also appreciate they can get quick resolution to those questions or issues because the company is decisive.

Act with a sense of authenticity—Companies committed to their customer and their online experience know it is a privilege when a customer follows them or reaches out. They also know their customers can tell when someone is trying to pull the wool over their eyes. Therefore, these companies choose an authentic voice online, one that speaks directly to their customer about things they value.

Provide "custom" service—Customer-centric companies work hard daily to create online experiences for their customers that they can't get anywhere else. They simplify things. They reach out to find out what's on their customers' minds, and then provide specific information to help them. They know who their customers are and what's important to them. They also respect their customers' space and don't spam them.

> Act with radical sincerity—Companies who value their customers will be quick to take responsibility for those not-so-perfect situations. This ties to their authenticity. The amazing thing that happens when a company acts with radical sincerity online is they get more committed followers because they show that not everyone is perfect.

Technology does not change the human experience. Whether you are interacting with your customers online or off, treating them with respect, and dignity will always give you the competitive advantage.

# Who's Really #1?

*"Treat employees like they make a difference and they will"*

~ Jim Goodnight

We've all experienced it. It could be in a shoe store at the mall, at the corner supermarket, or at a local restaurant. While trying to get serviced, we notice the gaggle of employees, clearly disgruntled, and overhear them speak badly about the business itself, and often management as well.

"Do you believe they do things this way? It is so stupid." "Did you hear that Fred really wants us to all punch the clock when we come in? That's ridiculous." "I've already started looking for another job. It is just miserable working here."

Now, that's not to say that there aren't workers that don't measure up to a business's standards and should be let go, immediately. There are plenty of those and likely always will be. But, there are also the workers who would really like to contribute, to make a difference, to *service the customer.* And they don't get the chance, or maybe more appropriately, aren't given the resources, help, and encouragement needed to make a difference.

We've all also seen, and hopefully have at our businesses, associates who go out of their way to do things the right way. They always run the extra mile to make sure that the customer is delighted. And we know instinctively that management and ownership value the contributions of those that show such great customer care. The best customer service organizations allow their associates to do what is best for the customer.

Herb Kelleher, founder of Southwest Airlines, once said, "If you create an environment where people truly participate, you don't need control. They know what needs to be done, and they do it. And the more that people will devote themselves to your cause on a voluntary basis, a willing basis, the fewer hierarchies and control mechanisms you need."

Supporting that kind of organization need not be difficult. It could be simple things like a thank-you note or a public praising. It could be team-building activities like off-site meetings or a night out bowling. It could be formal programs like employee of the month or best customer satisfaction score. Or, it could be, in every way, showing your gratitude to your employees and telling them how much you value their contributions to the overall success of the business. Appreciation never goes out of style.

You can't treat your frontlines poorly and expect your customers to be well taken care of. The essential laws of human nature just won't allow such a thing to happen in most cases. The retention of happy, engaged employees assures the retention of happy, satisfied, and engaged customers. Stephen Covey had it right when he said, "Always treat your employees exactly as you want them to treat your best customers." The Golden Rule still and always will apply. Everywhere.

Your employees are customers too. When they are happy and feel taken care of, they will go above and beyond for the customer every time, and even online.

In the past, employees, like customers, talked to friends and family about their work experiences. They kvetched with coworkers possibly at work, but after work.

Today, they can do this publicly on the social channels. They will find support in friends, family, and followers which can amplify their message. None of this is good for your company brand or for your customers.

We talked earlier about companies committed to customer service acting in faith instead of fear. Companies engaged in fear will strive to stifle their employee engagement on social. Usually, the outcome is more employee engagement. Companies acting in faith and who care for their employees in authentic ways don't have to have strict communication or social policies because their employees are happy.

When that happy employee takes to social, what do you think they share? Pictures from the company picnic, the award they received, or they may be praising another employee.

How do you think this affects your customers?

Happy and cared for employees not only spread the good cheer with their friends, family, and followers, but they infect customers. People see what they are saying, and they either feel good about doing business with the company, or if they are choosing which company to purchase from, your name will be at the top of the list. The more positive interactions they see from all employees, the better they feel about the company.

Starbucks uses the hashtag #tobeapartner on Twitter. It is fun to see how employees interact. It allows everyone to post what is happening at their stores, celebrate each other, and do it all publicly. Customers seeing these posts can't help but want to be part of the party. When they are tagged in a #tobeapartner post, they always share.

Taking care of employees takes on an even more important role since the advent of social. Do you know what your employees are saying online?

# The Magic Formula

*"I've learned that people will forget what you said, people will forget what you did, but people will never forget how you made them feel"*

~ Maya Angelou

The Holy Grail. The Silver Bullet. Pixie Dust. Winning the Lottery. Love Potion #9.

In every area of life, across all of our human endeavors, we are forever seeking that one thing that will make all of the difference. The Recipe. The Secret. The Magic Formula.

And yet, through all of our collective searching, The Answer remains the same, in every area. Always. People will (almost) always move away from situations where they do not feel understood, dismissed, or taken for granted. And conversely, they will (almost) always move toward, and stay with, situations where they feel valued, respected, and appreciated.

How you make your customers *feel*, based on solving each of their unique needs, will determine how well you build and retain long-term, satisfied, and loyal customers.

Modern technology is amazing. All of the ways we have to measure customer activity, satisfaction, and movement is truly incredible. And it will only continue to trend upward over time. The triumph of science over art. Big Brother comes to Big Business. Organizationally, we've all become more than somewhat obsessed with metrics.

But the ability to decipher trends and patterns will, in my opinion, always trail the face-to-face, belly-to-belly interactions that we have with our best customers and advocates. Humans are still humans, after all. And always will be. They cannot be reduced to an algorithm, a statistic, or a chart. And their impulsive, sometimes irrational and unpredictable, responses, based on our very "human" emotions, will continue to dictate choices, actions, and . . . orders.

The intangibles still sometimes count for more than the tangibles. As Albert Einstein famously said, "Not everything that counts can be counted, and not everything that can be counted counts."

If the ultimate goal is to attract, acquire, and retain customers, develop and deploy all of the sophisticated technological business development methods that you possibly can.

But above all else, make sure that you make your customers feel special.

One of the ways you can use technology to make customers feel special is to treat them like a VIP online.

What does this mean?

It means all that we've been talking about from showing up, to being authentic, to fessing up when you mess up.

It also means treating them special. This could be giving them the inside scoop, behind-the-scenes glimpses, or, in other words, give them something others who are not following you cannot get.

Are online relationships real relationships?

The answer is yes, when they are approached authentically. Companies who value their customers, however, do not solely rely on social to build and maintain their relationships. Instead, they use a combination of tactics where they engage with customers online, take it off-line, and bring it back online.

A great example is a company who recently attended a trade show. Four weeks prior, they authentically engaged with other exhibitors, potential customers, and existing customers. They used their social channels to build excitement about the trade show, as well as share information. They also asked a lot of questions to folks in the area about things to do outside of the trade show.

Once at the show, they had much more traffic than they had seen in the past. Many visitors were people who they had connected with prior to the show, but others were following the show's hashtag and saw their engagement. The goal for the show was to get one large client. They ended up getting *several* large clients, plus leads to future clients. It all started with their online engagement.

They didn't disappear after the show, however. They continued to engage through social and e-mail with people they met to strengthen their relationships and build future referral opportunities.

Social is the new phone call. When combined with face-to-face opportunities and done authentically, social can help you build and maintain long-lasting relationships.

# The 10 Commandments of Customer Service

*"Sales go up and down. Service stays forever"*

~ Jason Goldberg

1. Do understand the expectations of each individual customer
2. Do strive to exceed those expectations by providing custom service
3. Do apologize quickly and sincerely if you make a mistake
4. Do make it easy for customers to buy from you
5. Do make it easy for customers to return things to you if they change their minds
6. Do strive to develop an army of customers who are fanatics about advocating to their friends about you and your business
7. Do not ever think that "one-size-fits-all" service actually does
8. Do not think that customers will come back if you provide an average experience
9. Do not think that customers will accept you making the same mistake over and over again, and maybe not even twice
10. Do not ever take your customers for granted

# Epilogue
# The Six Pillars of Business Development

*"The loftier the building, the deeper must the foundation be laid"*

Thomas à Kempis

Business development is certainly a "lofty" goal. It is one that drives economic growth in a macroenvironment and creates both profits and sustainability in a micro-one. It is also, as many of us have come to find out, much more challenging to achieve in a social media world where many of the traditional rules have seemingly changed.

But have they really? Or, are there some principles and fundamentals that are truly eternal? Is it that the tactics and methods of delivery have, and will always continue to, evolve over time?

Great organizations are built on the effective coordination of marketing, sales, and customer service. When all three are in alignment, the finding, getting, and keeping of customers becomes much easier. No matter how technology, buying patterns, and tastes change, these will always be the six pillars on which to build your business development efforts.

Marketing

1. An unshakeable, long-term promise to yourself to use marketing efforts as the catalyst to attract and inform potential customers.

2. An open-minded willingness to always experiment with new marketing strategies and tactics to engage and educate your target audience.

Sales

3. The resolve to highly qualify each potential customer and create as many opportunities as possible that you consider to be an "ideal" fit for you and your organization.
4. The decision to create and follow an effective selling process that can convert as many of those potential opportunities as possible into customers.

Customer Service

5. An uncompromising determination to understand each of your customer's unique expectations.
6. An adamant commitment to provide a "custom" service experience and exceed expectations.

Build all your business development efforts with these pillars as your foundation and embrace the philosophy that they inspire. Do so and you will always generate the right opportunities and create happy, satisfied, loyal customers.

# About The Authors

Brian Butler is vice president of business development for The Allied Group, a leading provider of both sophisticated kitting & fulfillment services, as well as high-impact marketing communications and lead generation programs for the life science, higher education, and financial services industries. For the past 30 years, he has held various positions in marketing, sales, and customer service. In his current role, he is responsible for spearheading client acquisition efforts for the organization.

He is the author of ***Find 'Em, Get 'Em, Keep 'Em***—*Proven Strategies for Attracting, Acquiring and Retaining the Right Customers,* created from his diverse experiences in sales and marketing, and life.

In his speaking and training capacity, Brian has given numerous keynote addresses and presentations for organizations such as AARP, IBM, The American Yacht Charter Association, Atlas Travel International, and One Communications.

Brian holds a BS in marketing, graduating with honors from the University of Bridgeport, where he attended school on a two-sport athletic scholarship for soccer and baseball, and an MBA from Century University. He is a lifelong resident of Rhode Island.

Jen Vondenbrink is a nationally recognized authority on moving people outside their comfort zone. From her career with Starbucks Coffee Company, she learned coloring inside the lines isn't always a formula for growth. Today, she engages individuals and companies ready for change, especially when it comes to social media and e-mail marketing, as a business consultant, speaker, professional trainer, and author.

After receiving her marketing degree from Babson College, Jen went on to work for companies such as General Motors, Toyota, and Starbucks Coffee Company. Today, she blends her Fortune 500 experiences with her entrepreneurial knowledge to support businesses ready to grow. She has been recognized by both the Tri-Town Chamber of Commerce and the Commonwealth of Massachusetts for her commitment to education for the business community.

We hope you enjoyed *In Search of. . . Customers.*

For articles, updates, and more information,
please check out our website:

www.in-search-of-customers.com.

If you are interested in ordering additional copies of *In Search of. . . Customers* for your Sales, Marketing, or Customer Service Teams; have specific questions; or would like Brian Butler and/or Jen Vondenbrink to speak to your organization, please contact:

Brain Butler: bbutler@thealliedgrp.com

Jen Vondenbrink: jen@yourlifesimplified.com

You can find Brian's first book, *Find 'em Get 'em Keep 'em*
on Amazon.com

http://amzn.to/2mhvvId

You can order additional copies of *In Search of. . . Customers* on Amazon.com.

CPSIA information can be obtained
at www.ICGtesting.com
Printed in the USA
LVOW10s1021240617
539249LV00006B/298/P

9 781478 771395